Disaster Risk Management Series

Natural Disaster Hotspots
A Global Risk Analysis

by

Maxx Dilley,[1] Robert S. Chen,[2] Uwe Deichmann,[3]
Arthur L. Lerner-Lam,[4] and Margaret Arnold[5]
with Jonathan Agwe,[5] Piet Buys,[3] Oddvar Kjekstad,[6]
Bradfield Lyon,[1] and Gregory Yetman[2]

The World Bank
Hazard Management Unit
2005
Washington, D.C.

[1] International Research Institute for Climate Prediction (IRI), Columbia University
[2] Center for International Earth Science Information Network (CIESIN), Columbia University
[3] Development Economics Research Group (DECRG), The World Bank
[4] Center for Hazards and Risk Research (CHRR) and Lamont-Doherty Earth Observatory (LDEO), Columbia University
[5] Hazard Management Unit (HMU), The World Bank
[6] International Centre for Geohazards (ICG), Norwegian Geotechnical Institute (NGI)

Contents

Figures

Preface

As this volume goes to print, millions of people in Asia attempt to rebuild their lives and communities following the devastating earthquake and tsunami that occurred on December 26, 2004. The earthquake occurred off the coast of Sumatra, registering 9.0 on the Richter scale, and causing tsunami waves that swept through the Indian Ocean at a rate of 500-700 km per hour, devastating coastal areas of countries across South and Southeast Asia and East Africa. More than 220,000 people were killed, thousands more were injured, and millions affected. Damage to infrastructure, social systems, and the environment has been substantial. At the time of this writing, preliminary damage and needs assessments undertaken by the World Bank and other partners estimate the damages at nearly $6 billion for Indonesia, the Maldives, and Sri Lanka alone.

The tragic impacts and seeming enormity of this event have thrown many around the world into a state of disbelief. As shocking as the tsunami disaster is, however, it's important to remember that events of this magnitude have happened in other places around the world, and they will happen again. In 1984, persistent droughts in Ethiopia and Sudan killed 450,000. In Bangladesh in 1991, nearly 150,000 lives were taken by a cyclone. Hundreds of natural disasters, both large and small, occur each year. While the largest capture the attention of the global media, there are hundreds more events that we don't hear about. The cumulative effect of these smaller and medium-sized disasters have equally devastating impacts on developing countries: loss of development gains, torn communities, and increased impoverishment. The poor in these countries are consistently the most severely affected.

The Hotspots initiative began in 2001, when the World Bank's Disaster Management Facility (DMF), now the Hazard Management Unit (HMU), initiated discussions with the newly established Center for Hazards and Risk Research (CHRR) at Columbia University to discuss the possibility of a global-scale, multihazard risk analysis focused on identifying key "hotspots" where the risks of natural disasters are particularly high. The project would aim to provide information and methods to inform priorities for reducing disaster risk and making decisions on development investment. Discussions culminated in a jointly sponsored "brainstorming" workshop held at Columbia in September 2001 at which a small group of experts examined in depth whether such an analysis was feasible and worthwhile. A summary of the workshop and presentations is available on the ProVention Consortium Web site at: http://www.provention-consortium.org/conferences/highriskhotspots.htm.

Developed from that initial workshop, the Identification of Global Natural Disaster Risk Hotspots (Hotspots) project was implemented under the umbrella of the ProVention Consortium by World Bank staff from the HMU and the Development Economics Research Group (DECRG) and Columbia University staff from the CHRR, the Center for International Earth Science Information Network (CIESIN), the International Research Institute for Climate Prediction (IRI), and the Lamont-Doherty Earth Observatory (LDEO). The project has also benefited greatly from close collaboration with the Norwegian Geotechnical Institute (NGI), the United Nations Development Programme (UNDP), the United Nations Environment Programme (UNEP), the United Nations Office for the Coordination of Humanitarian Affairs (OCHA), the United Nations World Food Programme (WFP), the U.S. Geological Survey (USGS), the International Strategy for Disaster Reduction (ISDR), and other individuals and groups.

In November 2002, a second workshop was held at Columbia University involving experts on key natural hazards as well as potential case study authors. (For more information on this workshop, see http://www.proventionconsortium.org/conferences/high-riskhotspots2002.htm.) This workshop reviewed the initial plans and approaches under development by the core project staff, coordinated plans for the case studies, and obtained feedback from the World Bank and others, including the new director of the Earth Institute at Columbia University, Professor Jeffrey Sachs. This workshop led to the preparation of a revised work plan, including the addition of several new case study activities to the project. Intensive project work continued in 2003, culminating in a working meeting in December 2003 at which key results were reviewed and plans developed for the final project reports and dissemination of results. In March 2004, a review and synthesis meeting was held at the World Bank in Washington, D.C., where project results were presented to experts from the ISDR Working Group III on Vulnerability, Risk and Impacts; the World Bank; and other interested organizations.

This report contains the results of the global hotspots analysis as well as summaries of the case studies, which are being published as a separate volume. The list of case studies and contributors is provided in Table 8.1. This publication does not examine tsunami hazard risk, as comprehensive data sets were not available during the course of the study. However, plans are being made to include an analysis of tsunami-related risks in a subsequent phase of hotspots research.

The project team wishes to thank the HMU—especially its former manager, Alcira Kreimer—for her strong support, guidance, and encouragement throughout this challenging project. We thank Maryvonne Plessis-Fraissard, Director of the Transport and Urban Development Department, and Eleoterio Codato, Sector Manager for Urban Development, for their support of the initiative. We thank Maria Eugenia Quintero and Zoe Trohanis at the HMU for their technical and organizational contributions to the project. We especially thank the United Kingdom's Department for International Development (DFID) and Norwegian Ministry of Foreign Affairs for their interest and financial support. We are grateful to the CHRR, the Earth Institute, and the Lamont-Doherty Earth Observatory of Columbia University for

providing complementary funding of the project and their support of the Caracas case study.

The Hotspots project benefited enormously from interactions with the project on Reducing Disaster Risk, a collaborative effort involving UNDP, UNEP, and others. We especially thank Yasmin Aysan, Pascal Peduzzi, Andrew Maskrey, and Ron Witt for their willingness to exchange data, methods, and ideas. These two projects share a common approach with regard to analysis of disaster risk and vulnerability. Pablo Recalde played a key role in organizing WFP participation in the project and case studies. We also acknowledge the support of the U.S. Agency for International Development (USAID) for the Tana River case study.

We thank Kathy Boyer for her extensive help with project management and implementation, especially with regard to the case studies. We very much appreciate the tireless efforts of Piet Buys of DECRG and Greg Yetman and Kobi Abayomi of CIESIN to access, transform, and analyze the wide range of global data used in this project. We gratefully acknowledge the extensive administrative and organizational support provided by Stacey Gander of the CHRR and Jennifer Mulvey, Ed Ortiz, and Hannia Smith of CIESIN. We also thank our colleagues within the Earth Institute at Columbia University for their extensive inputs and guidance on a wide range of issues, both organizational and technical. These individuals include Deborah Balk, George Deodatis, Klaus Jacob, Upmanu Lall, Marc Levy, Brad Lyon, Roberta Balstad Miller, Chet Ropelewski, Jeffrey Sachs, Andrew Smyth, Angeletti Taramelli, Jeff Weissel, and Lareef Zubair. We are grateful to Matt Barlow, Klaus Jacob, Oddvar Kjekstad, and Sylvia Mosquera for their helpful reviews of the final draft. Of course, the opinions, conclusions, and recommendations provided in this report are those of the authors and not necessarily those of the World Bank, the Trustees of Columbia University in the City of New York, our sponsors, partners, or colleagues.

Hotspots aims to provide a tool to get ahead of the disaster trend by highlighting areas that are most vulnerable to a number of hazards. We hope that development agencies and policymakers will use the information to plan ahead for disasters and minimize their impacts. This implies understanding the risk facing a particular community, city, or region, and integrating this understanding into development planning decisions. The knowledge and affordable technologies *do* exist to allow even low-income countries to significantly reduce the devastating social and economic impacts caused by such hazards as droughts, floods and earthquakes that are part of the natural cycle of so many countries. The triggers may be natural, but responsibility for the impacts of disasters belongs to all of us.

Maxx Dilley, IRI
Robert S. Chen, CIESIN
Uwe Deichmann, DECRG, World Bank
Art Lerner-Lam, CHRR/LDEO
Margaret Arnold, HMU, World Bank

Acronyms and Abbreviations

CAS	Country Assistance Strategy
CHRR	Center for Hazards and Risk Research
CIESIN	Center for International Earth Science Information Network
CRED	Centre for Research on the Epidemiology of Disasters
DECRG	Development Economics Research Group
DFID	UK Department for International Development
DMF	Disaster Management Facility (now HMU)
DRI	Disaster Risk Index
ECLAC	Economic Commission for Latin America and the Caribbean
EM-DAT	Emergency Events Database
ENSO	El Niño-Southern Oscillation
ERL	Emergency Reconstruction Loan
FTS	Financial Tracking System
GDP	Gross domestic product
GIS	Geographic Information System
GPW	Gridded Population of the World
GSHAP	Global Seismic Hazard Program
HMU	Hazard Management Unit
ICG	International Centre for Geohazards
IFPRI	International Food Policy Research Institute
IFRC	International Federation of the Red Cross
IRI	International Research Institute for Climate Prediction
ISDR	International Strategy for Disaster Reduction
LDEO	Lamont-Doherty Earth Observatory
NGDC	National Geophysical Data Center
NGI	Norwegian Geotechnical Institute
NIMA	National Imagery and Mapping Agency
NRC	National Research Council
OCHA	Office for the Coordination of Humanitarian Affairs
pga	Peak ground acceleration
PNG	Papua New Guinea
PPP	Purchasing power parity
PreView	Project of Risk Evaluation, Vulnerability, Information and Early Warning
SRTM	Shuttle Radar Topographic Mission
UNDP	United Nations Development Programme

UNEP   United Nations Environment Programme
USGS   United States Geological Survey
VEI   Volcanic Explosivity Index
VMAP(0)   Vector Map Level 0
WASP   Weighted Anomaly of Standardized Precipitation
WFP   World Food Programme
WRI   World Resources Institute

Chapter 1
Executive Summary

Earthquakes, floods, drought, and other natural hazards continue to cause tens of thousands of deaths, hundreds of thousands of injuries, and billions of dollars in economic losses each year around the world. The Emergency Events Database (EM-DAT), a global disaster database maintained by the Centre for Research on the Epidemiology of Disasters (CRED) in Brussels, records upwards of 600 disasters globally each year (http://www.cred.be). Disaster frequency appears to be increasing. Disasters represent a major source of risk for the poor and wipe out development gains and accumulated wealth in developing countries.

As the recognition grows that natural disaster risk must be addressed as a development issue rather than one strictly of humanitarian assistance, so must our efforts to develop the tools to effectively mainstream disaster risk management into development activities. This project has attempted to develop a global, synoptic view of the major natural hazards, assessing risks of multiple disaster-related outcomes and focusing in particular on the degree of overlap between areas exposed to multiple hazards. The overall goal is to identify geographic areas of highest disaster risk potential in order to better inform development efforts.

Project Approach

In this report we assess the risks of two disaster-related outcomes: mortality and economic losses. We estimate risk levels by combining hazard exposure with historical vulnerability for two indicators of elements at risk—gridded population and gross domestic product (GDP) per unit area—for six major natural hazards: earthquakes, volcanoes, landslides, floods, drought, and cyclones. By calculating relative risks for grid cells rather than for countries as a whole, we are able to estimate risk levels at subnational scales.

The global analysis is limited by issues of scale as well as by the availability and quality of data. For a number of hazards, we had only 15- to 25-year records of events for the entire globe and relatively crude spatial information for locating these events. Data on historical disaster losses, and particularly on economic losses, are also limited.

While the data are inadequate for understanding the *absolute* levels of risk posed by any specific hazard or combination of hazards, they are adequate for identifying areas that are at relatively higher single- or multiple-hazard risk. In other words, we do not feel that the data are sufficiently reliable to estimate, for example, the total mortality risk from flooding, earthquakes, and drought over a specified period. Nevertheless, we can identify those areas that are at *higher* risk of flood losses than others and at *higher* risk of earthquake damage than others, or at *higher* risk of both. We can also assess in general terms the *exposure* and *potential magnitude* of losses to people and their assets in these areas. Such information can inform a range of disaster prevention and preparedness measures, including prioritization of resources, targeting of more localized and detailed risk assessments, implementation of risk-based disaster management and emergency response strategies, and development of long-term land use plans and multihazard risk management strategies.

A set of case studies explores risks from particular hazards or for localized areas in more detail, using the same theoretical framework as the global analysis. We hope that in addition to providing interesting and useful results, the global analysis and case studies will stimulate additional research, particularly at national and local levels, which will be increasingly linked to policy making and practice in disaster risk reduction.

Within the constraints summarized above, we developed three indexes of disaster risk:

1. Mortality risks, assessed for global gridded population
2. Risks of total economic losses, assessed for global gridded GDP per unit area
3. Risks of economic losses expressed as a proportion of the GDP per unit area for each grid cell

Risks of both mortality and economic losses are calculated as a function of the expected hazard frequency and expected losses per hazard event. We obtained global hazard data on cyclones, drought, earthquakes, floods, landslides, and volcanoes from a variety of sources. The global hazard data sets were improved upon or, in the case of droughts and landslides, created specifically for the analysis. Vulnerability was estimated by obtaining hazard-specific mortality and economic loss rates for World Bank regions and country wealth classes within them based on 20 years of historical loss data from the EM-DAT database.

We masked out low-population and nonagricultural areas where risks of losses are negligible. After calculating the expected losses for each remaining grid cell, we ranked the grid cells and classified them into deciles (10 classes composed of roughly equal numbers of cells). Cells falling into the highest three deciles for either mortality or economic losses are considered *disaster risk hotspots*.

Key Findings of the Global Analysis

Among the findings are that on the order of 25 million square kilometers (km²) (about 19 percent of the Earth's land area) and 3.4 billion people (more than half of the world's population) are relatively highly exposed to at least one hazard. Some 3.8 million square kilometers and 790 million people are relatively highly exposed to at least two hazards. About 0.5 million square kilometers and 105 million people are relatively highly exposed to three or more hazards (Figure 1.1). In some countries, large percentages of the population reside in hazard-prone areas (Table 1.1).

The fact that some areas of the world are subject to multiple hazards will not surprise many residents of those areas, but what this analysis reveals is the extent to which, at global and regional scales, there is substantial overlap between different types of hazards and population concentrations. The world's geophysical hazards—earthquakes and volcanoes—tend to cluster along fault boundaries characterized by mountainous terrain. Hazards driven mainly by hydro-meteorological processes—floods, cyclones, and landslides—strongly affect the eastern coastal regions of the major continents as well as some interior regions of North and South America, Europe, and Asia. Drought is more widely dispersed across the semiarid tropics. The areas subject to both geophysically- and hydro-meteorologically-driven hazards fall primarily in East and South Asia and in Central America and western South America. Many of these areas are also more densely populated and developed than average, leading to high potential for casualties and economic losses. Of particular concern in these areas are possible interactions between different hazards, for example, landslides triggered by cyclones and flooding, or earthquakes that damage dams and reservoirs needed for drought and flood protection.

The global analysis supports the view that disaster risk management is a core issue of development. Comparing Figures 1.1 and 1.2a illustrates the degree to which exposure to hazards in developed countries has *not* led to relatively high mortality in the past two decades in these areas. Areas of Europe and North America that are highly exposed to natural hazards as shown in Figure 1.1, for example, have not experienced correspondingly high mortality from these hazards over the past two decades. The United States is noteworthy in that more than one-third of its population lives in hazard-prone areas but only 1 percent of its land area ranks high in mortality risk.

Figure 1.2 shows the types of hazards for which each grid cell appeared in the top three deciles of the global risk distribution for mortality (a) and economic losses (b and c). Figure 1.2b shows that areas at high risk of economic losses are more widely distributed in industrial and lower-middle-income countries than areas of high mortality risk. In addition to portions of Central America and East and South Asia, large areas of the eastern Mediterranean and Middle East appear at high

Figure 1.1. Global Distribution of Areas Highly Exposed to One or More Hazards, by Hazard Type

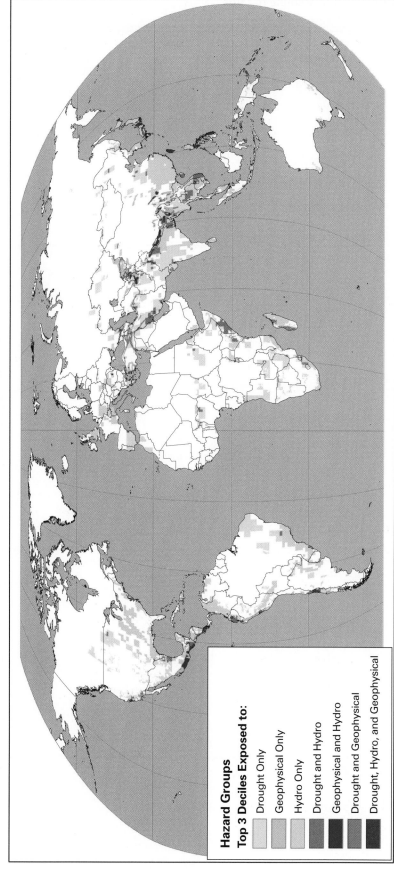

Hazard Groups
Top 3 Deciles Exposed to:
- Drought Only
- Geophysical Only
- Hydro Only
- Drought and Hydro
- Geophysical and Hydro
- Drought and Geophysical
- Drought, Hydro, and Geophysical

Note: Geophysical hazards include earthquakes and volcanoes; hydrological hazards include floods, cyclones, and landslides.

Table 1.1. Countries Most Exposed to Multiple Hazards

a) Three or more hazards (top 15 based on land area)

Country	Percent of Total Area Exposed	Percent of Population Exposed	Max. Number of Hazards	Country	Percent of Total Area Exposed	Percent of Population Exposed	Max. Number of Hazards
Taiwan, China	73.1	73.1	4	Vietnam	8.2	5.1	3
Costa Rica	36.8	41.1	4	Solomon Islands	7.0	4.9	3
Vanuatu	28.8	20.5	3	Nepal	5.3	2.6	3
Philippines	22.3	36.4	5	El Salvador	5.1	5.2	3
Guatemala	21.3	40.8	5	Tajikistan	5.0	1.0	3
Ecuador	13.9	23.9	5	Panama	4.4	2.9	3
Chile	12.9	54.0	4	Nicaragua	3.0	22.2	3
Japan	10.5	15.3	4				

b) Two or more hazards (top 60 based on land area)

Country	Percent of Total Area Exposed	Percent of Population Exposed	Max. Number of Hazards	Country	Percent of Total Area Exposed	Percent of Population Exposed	Max. Number of Hazards
St. Kitts and Nevis	100.0	100.0	2	Mexico	16.5	9.6	4
Macao, China	100.0	100.0	2	Korea, Dem. People's Rep. of	16.4	13.5	3
Antigua and Barbuda	100.0	100.0	2				
Hong Kong, China	100.0	100.0	2	Lao People's Dem. Rep. of	15.2	12.6	3
Taiwan, China	99.1	98.9	4				
Vanuatu	80.8	75.6	3	Turkey	15.1	11.3	3
Costa Rica	80.4	69.2	4	Panama	15.0	12.6	3
Philippines	62.2	73.8	5	Swaziland	14.3	14.2	2
Nepal	60.5	51.6	3	Nicaragua	12.4	49.8	3
Guatemala	56.6	83.4	5	Afghanistan	11.1	29.5	3
Korea, Rep. of	53.0	53.6	2	Myanmar	10.7	10.4	4
Ecuador	47.6	74.6	5	India	10.5	10.9	4
Réunion	45.7	45.7	2	Lesotho	10.3	3.7	2
Vietnam	45.1	38.7	3	Iceland	9.4	4.8	2
Somalia	43.1	53.8	2	Colombia	8.9	7.5	3
South Africa	43.1	46.9	2	China	8.4	15.7	3
Japan	38.1	48.4	4	Kyrgyz Rep.	8.3	5.8	2
Cayman Islands	36.8	45.6	2	Dominica	8.1	6.2	2
Bangladesh	35.6	32.9	4	Peru	7.4	26.3	3
El Salvador	32.4	39.7	3	Iraq	7.3	9.6	3
Cambodia	27.9	4.4	3	Cuba	6.6	4.3	2
Chile	26.2	62.6	4	Papua New Guinea	5.9	6.4	3
Thailand	25.2	17.7	2	Jamaica	5.7	7.2	2
Fiji	23.2	29.0	2	Pakistan	5.6	18.2	2
Tajikistan	23.2	9.5	3	Indonesia	4.5	14.1	3
Solomon Islands	22.8	16.6	3	New Zealand	4.3	1.7	3
Madagascar	20.2	9.9	2	United Arab Emirates	4.1	6.8	2
Bhutan	20.1	29.2	4	Armenia	3.1	1.5	3
Georgia	17.4	5.9	3	Mongolia	2.8	0.7	2
Iran, Islamic Rep. of	17.1	22.2	4	Nigeria	2.7	6.7	2
Kenya	16.9	8.8	2	United States	2.6	11.2	4

Figure 1.2. Global Distribution of Highest Risk Disaster Hotspots by Hazard Type
a) Mortality Risks

High Mortality Risk
Top 3 Deciles at Risk from:

- Drought Only
- Geophysical Only
- Hydro Only
- Drought and Hydro
- Geophysical and Hydro
- Drought and Geophysical
- Drought, Hydro, and Geophysical

Note: Geophysical hazards include earthquakes and volcanoes; hydrological hazards include floods, cyclones, and landslides.

Natural Disaster Hotspots: A Global Risk Analysis

Figure 1.2. Global Distribution of Highest Risk Disaster Hotspots by Hazard Type
b) Total Economic Loss Risks

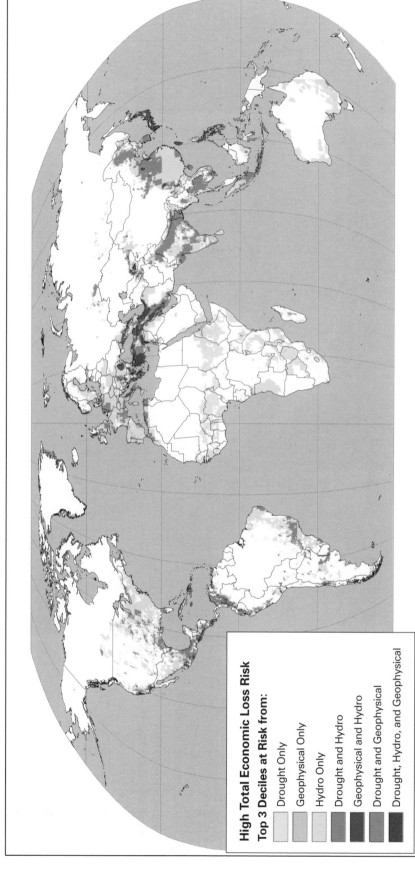

High Total Economic Loss Risk
Top 3 Deciles at Risk from:

- Drought Only
- Geophysical Only
- Hydro Only
- Drought and Hydro
- Geophysical and Hydro
- Drought and Geophysical
- Drought, Hydro, and Geophysical

Note: Geophysical hazards include earthquakes and volcanoes; hydrological hazards include floods, cyclones, and landslides.

Figure 1.2. Global Distribution of Highest Risk Disaster Hotspots by Hazard Type
c) Economic Loss Risks as a Proportion of GDP Per Unit Area

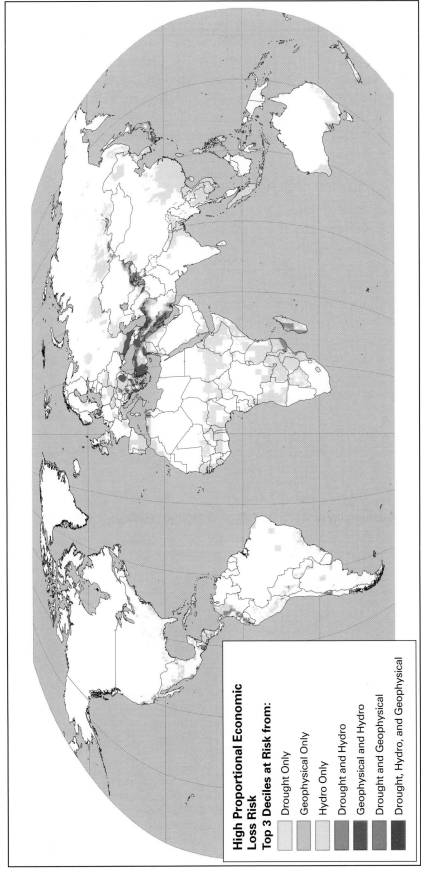

High Proportional Economic Loss Risk
Top 3 Deciles at Risk from:

- Drought Only
- Geophysical Only
- Hydro Only
- Drought and Hydro
- Geophysical and Hydro
- Drought and Geophysical
- Drought, Hydro, and Geophysical

Note: Geophysical hazards include earthquakes and volcanoes; hydrological hazards include floods, cyclones, and landslides.

risk of loss from multiple hazards. These regions still rank high when the risk is recalculated by dividing the losses per grid cell by each grid cell's GDP estimate (Figure 1.2c). In contrast, much of Europe and the United States no longer rank among the highest risk areas when grid cells are ranked according to losses as a proportion of GDP.

The statistics also suggest that future disasters will continue to impose high costs on human and economic development. In 35 countries, more than 1 in 20 residents lives in an area identified as relatively high in mortality risk from three or more hazards (Table 1.2a). More than 90 countries have more than 10 percent of their total population in areas at relatively high mortality risk from two or more hazards (Table 1.2b and Figure 1.3). And 160 countries have more than one-fourth of their total population in areas at relatively high mortality risk from one or more hazards (Figure 1.4). Similarly, many of the areas at higher risk of loss from multiple hazards are associated with higher-than-average densities of GDP, leading to a relatively high degree of exposure of economically productive areas (Figures 1.5 and 1.6).

Until vulnerability, and consequently risks, are reduced, countries with high proportions of population or GDP in hotspots are especially likely to incur repeated disaster-related losses and costs. Comparison of these maps with data on relief and reconstruction costs is instructive in this regard. Data on relief costs associated with natural disasters from 1992 to 2003 are available from the Financial Tracking System (FTS) of the United Nations Office for the Coordination of Humanitarian Affairs (OCHA) (http://www.reliefweb.int/fts/). Total relief costs over this period are US$2.5 billion. Of this, US$2 billion went to just 20 countries, primarily for disasters involving the following hazards (listed in order of magnitude of the relief amount allocated): China (earthquakes and floods); India (earthquakes, floods, and storms); Bangladesh (floods); the Arab Republic of Egypt (earthquakes); Mozambique (floods); Turkey (earthquakes); Afghanistan (drought and earthquakes); El Salvador (earthquakes); Kenya (drought and floods); the Islamic Republic of Iran (earthquakes); Pakistan (drought and floods); Indonesia (drought, earthquakes, and floods); Peru (earthquakes and floods); Democratic Republic of Congo (volcanoes); Poland (floods); Vietnam (floods and storms); Colombia (earthquakes); Venezuela (floods); Tajikistan (droughts and floods); and Cambodia (floods). All of these countries except Egypt have more than half of their population in areas

Table 1.2. Countries at Relatively High Mortality Risk from Multiple Hazards
a) Three or more hazards (top 35 based on population)

Country	Percent of Total Area at Risk	Percent of Population in Areas at Risk	Country	Percent of Total Area at Risk	Percent of Population at Risk
Taiwan, China	90.2	95.1	Madagascar	6.3	24.8
El Salvador	51.7	77.7	Trinidad and Tobago	10.0	23.5
Costa Rica	38.2	77.1	Ecuador	3.6	21.4
Philippines	45.6	72.6	Bhutan	10.5	18.8
Dominica	70.8	71.1	Chile	1.0	18.7
Antigua and Barbuda	46.2	69.5	Malawi	5.5	12.9
Guatemala	28.8	69.4	Solomon Islands	0.1	12.0
Japan	23.2	69.4	Mexico	4.4	10.8
Dominican Rep.	33.7	66.0	Fiji	4.1	9.4
Jamaica	40.5	58.8	Albania	4.0	8.6
Nicaragua	4.4	42.7	Cuba	3.5	8.5
Indonesia	4.4	40.1	Samoa	0.7	8.3
Comoros	39.6	32.0	Afghanistan	0.8	8.1
Honduras	18.1	31.8	Pakistan	1.4	5.9
Nepal	31.9	28.0	Venezuela	0.9	5.6
Bangladesh	30.0	26.2	Cameroon	1.1	5.5
Colombia	1.8	25.9	Panama	2.6	5.1
Mozambique	4.7	25.5			

Table 1.2. Countries at Relatively High Mortality Risk from Multiple Hazards

b) Two or more hazards (top 96 based on population)

Country	Percent of Total Area at Risk	Percent of Population in Areas at Risk	Country	Percent of Total Area at Risk	Percent of Population at Risk
Bangladesh	97.1	97.7	Afghanistan	7.2	46.0
Nepal	80.2	97.4	Georgia	19.2	44.0
Dominican Rep.	97.3	96.8	Cameroon	9.2	42.0
Burundi	96.3	96.6	Fiji	20.0	42.0
Haiti	93.4	96.5	St. Vincent and Grenadines	41.6	41.6
Taiwan, China	92.5	95.5	Mexico	15.1	41.3
Malawi	70.8	95.3	Togo	61.2	39.3
El Salvador	83.0	92.6	St. Kitts and Nevis	31.8	39.1
Honduras	64.5	91.5	Zimbabwe	10.1	39.0
Guatemala	54.9	89.5	Congo,Rep. Of	1.9	38.8
Philippines	76.6	88.6	Benin	37.2	38.6
Costa Rica	53.6	86.1	Belize	19.8	38.2
Trinidad and Tobago	63.4	85.1	Sierra Leone	13.0	35.7
Japan	34.7	84.0	United States	1.1	35.1
Antigua and Barbuda	54.5	82.0	China	10.6	33.4
Dominica	84.7	82.0	Romania	14.4	33.3
Nicaragua	38.1	81.9	Uzbekistan	2.5	30.6
South Africa	12.1	78.7	Mali	2.9	29.6
Cuba	87.0	77.5	Lebanon	19.2	29.2
Niger	14.0	76.4	Sudan	5.0	28.8
Korea, Dem. People's Rep. of	58.5	72.8	Tajikistan	5.8	28.2
Vietnam	59.3	71.4	India	21.9	27.2
Ethiopia	29.9	69.3	United Kingdom	7.9	27.0
Nigeria	47.5	68.8	Liechtenstein	23.1	26.6
Chile	5.3	68.3	Uganda	27.5	26.6
Ecuador	20.3	67.2	Canada	0.04	25.3
Korea, Rep. of	25.2	66.7	Syrian Arab Rep.	8.0	24.9
Colombia	12.8	66.3	Turkey	12.6	24.7
Kenya	29.0	63.4	Bolivia	0.6	24.7
Burkina Faso	35.1	61.7	Lao People's Dem. Rep.	9.1	22.4
Bhutan	31.2	60.8	New Zealand	0.8	22.4
Venezuela	6.7	60.1	Ireland	0.6	21.9
Indonesia	10.6	59.3	Congo, Dem. Rep. of	2.5	21.6
Mozambique	16.9	58.9	Chad	2.7	20.5
Jamaica	40.5	58.8	Central African Rep.	0.5	19.7
Guam	23.8	58.5	Jordan	3.0	17.7
Peru	5.7	57.5	Yugoslavia Fed. Rep. (Serbia/Montenegro)	17.1	17.5
Albania	33.4	56.7			
Madagascar	15.7	56.0	Myanmar	4.5	16.8
Barbados	54.9	54.9	Angola	0.2	14.8
Comoros	59.0	54.2	Rwanda	13.3	14.2
Tanzania	27.7	53.7	Panama	9.3	14.1
Somalia	15.4	53.3	Samoa	1.4	13.9
Senegal	10.1	52.9	Macedonia, FYR	22.4	13.7
Grenada	52.1	52.1	Kyrgyz Rep.	2.3	13.2
Lesotho	52.4	50.5	Solomon Islands	0.1	12.0
Montserrat	50.3	50.3	Ghana	15.2	11.6
Pakistan	22.8	49.6	Thailand	2.6	10.7
Iran, Islamic Rep. of	14.3	46.6			

Figure 1.3. Proportion of National Population In Highest Risk Areas from Two or More Hazards (Mortality)

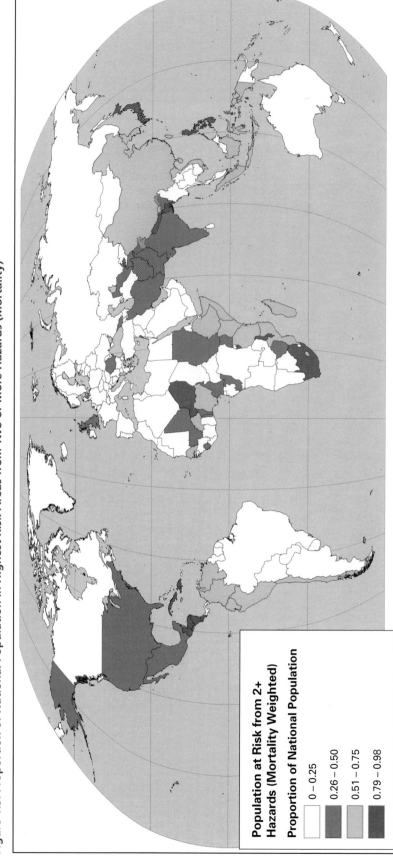

Population at Risk from 2+ Hazards (Mortality Weighted)
Proportion of National Population

- 0 – 0.25
- 0.26 – 0.50
- 0.51 – 0.75
- 0.79 – 0.98

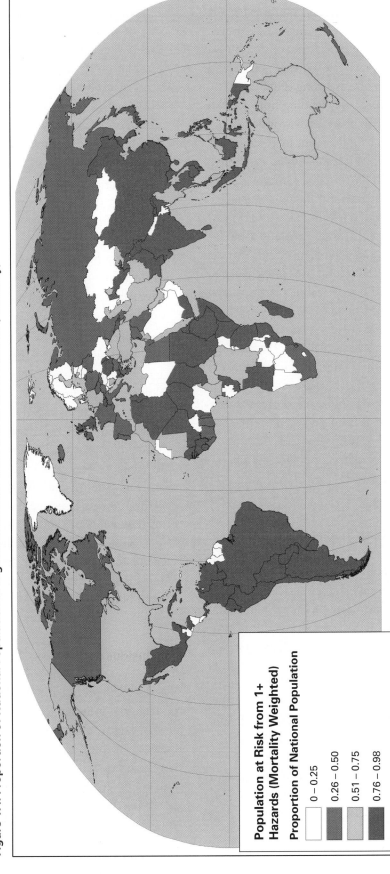

Figure 1.4. Proportion of National Population In Highest Risk Areas from One or More Hazards (Mortality)

Population at Risk from 1+ Hazards (Mortality Weighted)
Proportion of National Population

0 – 0.25

0.26 – 0.50

0.51 – 0.75

0.76 – 0.98

at relatively high risk from one or more hazards (Figure 1.4). The countries subject to multiple hazards in this list also are among those countries with at least one-fourth of their populations in areas at risk from two or more hazards (Figure 1.3). The correspondence with economic losses is not quite as strong (Figure 1.6).

Total World Bank emergency lending from 1980 to 2003 was US$14.4 billion (http://www.worldbank.org/hazards). Of this, US$12 billion went to 20 countries, primarily for the following hazards (listed in order of highest loan amount): India (drought, earthquakes, and storms); Turkey (earthquakes and floods); Bangladesh (floods and storms); Mexico (earthquakes and floods); Argentina (floods); Brazil (floods); Poland (floods); Colombia (earthquakes and floods); the Islamic Republic of Iran (earthquakes); Honduras (floods and storms); China (earthquakes and floods); Chile (earthquakes); Zimbabwe (drought); the Dominican Republic (storms); El Salvador (earthquakes); Algeria (earthquakes and floods); Ecuador (earthquakes and floods; Mozambique (drought and floods); the Philippines (earthquakes); and Vietnam (floods). All of these countries except Poland have half of their population in areas at relatively high mortality risk from one or more hazards (Figure 1.4), and all of them have at least half of their GDP in areas of relatively high economic risk from one or more hazards (Figure 1.6).

Key Findings of the Case Studies

Recognizing the limitations of the global analysis, we undertook a number of case studies designed to investigate the potential of the hotspots approach at regional, national, and subnational scales, drawing on more detailed and reliable data sources as well as on expert knowledge concerning specific hazards and regions. Three case studies addressed specific hazards: storm surges, landslides, and drought. Three case studies addressed regional multihazard situations: Sri Lanka, the Tana River basin in Kenya, and the city of Caracas, Venezuela.

The following are the key findings from the case studies:

1. *Scale matters.* Geographic areas that are identified as hotspots at the global scale may have a highly variable spatial distribution of risk at finer scales.
2. *Scale affects data availability and quality.* Hazard, exposure, and vulnerability data are available at subnational resolutions for individual countries and even cities, as the analyses for Sri Lanka and Caracas show. More comprehensive, finer resolution, and better quality data permit more complete, accurate, and reliable identification of multihazard hotspots.
3. *Scale affects the utility of the results.* Better data resolution and a richer set of variables contribute to results that are more relevant for risk management planning at the national to local scale, as illustrated in the case study from Caracas. This is highly important, as decisions made at the local and national scales have perhaps the greatest potential to affect risk levels directly, whether positively or negatively.
4. *The global- and local-scale analyses are complementary.* In some instances, national-to-local level risk assessors and planners may be able to "downscale" global data for finer scale risk assessment to compensate for a lack of local data. Ideally, however, global analyses would be scaled up—generalized from more detailed, finer scale data. In practice, many barriers still remain. The global infrastructure for systematically assembling and integrating relevant data sets for disaster risk assessment at multiple scales remains inadequate. Nonetheless, the fact that relevant data sets can be obtained and integrated at various scales creates the hope that one day data can be collected and shared routinely to improve disaster risk assessment both globally and locally.

Conclusions and the Way Forward

The Hotspots project has created an initial picture of the location and characteristics of disaster hotspots: areas at relatively high risk from one or more natural hazards. The findings of the analysis support the view that disasters will continue to impose high costs on human and economic development, and that disaster risk should be managed as an integral part of development planning rather than thought of strictly as a human-

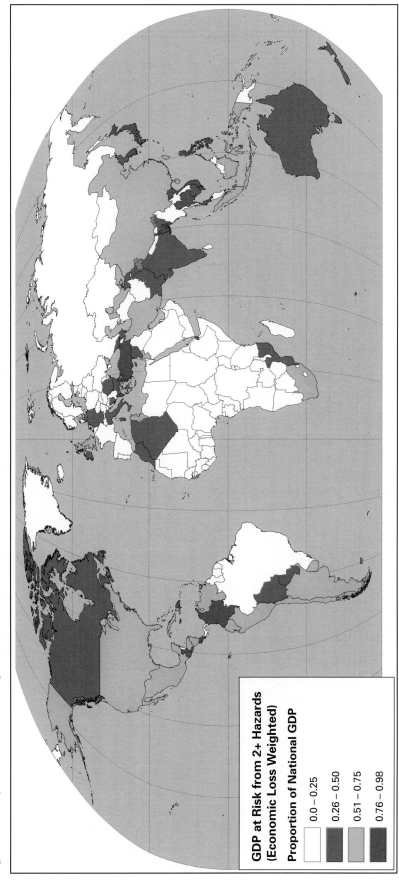

Figure 1.5. Proportion of GDP In Highest Risk Areas from Two or More Hazards (Economic Losses)

GDP at Risk from 2+ Hazards
(Economic Loss Weighted)

Proportion of National GDP

0.0 – 0.25
0.26 – 0.50
0.51 – 0.75
0.76 – 0.98

Figure 1.6. Proportion of GDP In Highest Risk Areas from One or More Hazards (Economic Losses)

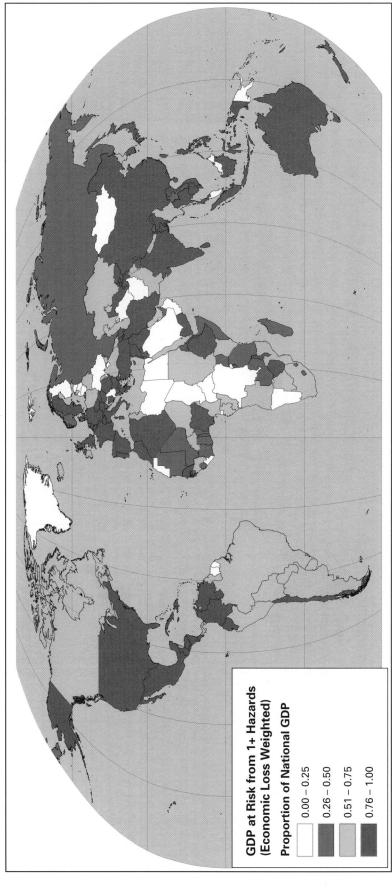

itarian issue. The following paragraphs detail how disaster risk information can be useful for development policy and decision makers, and how it can be further developed in order to increase its usefulness.

The Costs of Disaster Risks

The combination of human and economic losses, plus the additional costs of relief, rehabilitation, and reconstruction, make disasters an economic as well as a humanitarian issue. Until vulnerability, and consequently risks, are reduced, countries with high proportions of population or GDP in hotspots are especially likely to incur repeated disaster-related losses and costs. Disaster risks, therefore, deserve serious consideration as an issue for sustainable development in high-risk areas.

The significance of high mortality and economic loss risks for socioeconomic development extends well beyond the initial direct losses to the population and economy during disasters. Covariate losses accompanying mortality, for example, include partial or total loss of household assets, lost income, and lost productivity. Widespread disaster-related mortality can affect households and communities for years, decades, and even generations.

In addition to mortality and its long-term consequences, both direct and indirect economic losses must be considered (ECLAC and the World Bank 2003). Direct losses are losses to assets, whereas indirect losses are the losses that accrue while productive assets remain damaged or destroyed. During disasters, both direct and indirect losses accumulate across the social, productive, and infrastructure sectors. The pattern of losses depends on the type of hazard and the affected sectors' vulnerabilities to the hazard. In large disasters, cumulative losses across sectors can have macroeconomic impacts.

Disasters impose costs in addition to human and economic losses. Costs include expenditures for disaster relief and recovery and for rehabilitation and reconstruction of damaged and destroyed assets. In major disasters, meeting these additional costs can require external financing or international humanitarian assistance. Disaster relief costs drain development resources from productive investments to support consumption over short periods. Emergency loans have questionable value as vehicles for long-term investment and contribute to country indebtedness without necessarily improving economic growth or reducing poverty. As disasters continue to occur, high-risk countries will continue to need high levels of humanitarian relief and recovery lending unless their vulnerability is reduced.

Implications for Decision Making

The Hotspots analysis has implications for development investment planning, disaster preparedness, and loss prevention. The highest risk areas are those in which disasters are expected to occur most frequently and losses are expected to be highest. This provides a rational basis for prioritizing risk-reduction efforts and highlights areas where risk management is most needed.

International development organizations are key stakeholders with respect to the global analysis. The analysis provides a scientific basis for understanding where risks are highest and why, as well as a methodological framework for regional- and local-scale analysis. The identified risks then can be evaluated further using more detailed data in the context of a region's or country's overall development strategy and priorities. This would serve development institutions and the countries in several ways to facilitate the development of better-informed investment strategies and activities.

Assistance Strategies. A development institution such as the World Bank may use the analysis at the global and/or regional level to identify countries that are at higher risk of disasters and "flag" them as priorities to ensure that disaster risk management is addressed in the development of a Country Assistance Strategy (CAS). While in some countries there can be a seemingly long list of urgent priorities to address in a CAS—e.g., reducing extreme poverty, fighting HIV/AIDS, promoting education, achieving macroeconomic stability—managing disaster risk should be considered an integral part of the development planning to protect the investments made rather than as a stand-alone agenda. The CAS should consider the consequences of unmitigated disaster risk in terms of possible tradeoffs with long-term socioeconomic goals.

Sector Investment Operations. In high-risk regions and countries, it is particularly important to protect investments from damage or loss, either by limiting hazard exposure or by reducing vulnerability. Risks of damage and loss should also be taken into account when estimating economic returns during project preparation. Investment project preparation, particularly in the high-risk areas identified in the global analysis, would benefit from including a risk assessment as a standard practice. This report's theory and methods can be translated easily into terms of reference for such assessments. Such assessments should identify probable hazards, as well as their spatial distribution and temporal characteristics (including return periods), and should evaluate vulnerabilities to the identified hazards that should be addressed in the project design.

Risk Reduction Operations. In high-risk countries and areas within countries, repeated, large-scale loss events can harm economic performance (Benson and Clay 2004). It may be impossible to achieve development goals such as poverty alleviation in these areas without concerted efforts to reduce recurrent losses. Increasingly, risk and loss reduction are being seen as investments in themselves, and disaster-prone countries are demonstrating a willingness to undertake projects in which disaster and loss reduction are the principal aims. Such projects can include both hard and soft components: measures to reduce the vulnerability and exposure of infrastructure, as well as emergency funds and institutional, policy and capacity-building measures designed to increase the abilities of countries to manage disaster risks.

Contingency Financing. Emergency recovery and reconstruction needs after a major disaster may create a high demand for emergency financing. While such loans are usually appraised and approved relatively quickly, at times there can be delays in disbursing the funds, which increase the social and economic impacts of the disaster. Advance planning for recovery and resource allocation would allow for better targeting of

resources toward investments that would restore economic activity quickly and relieve human suffering. This report's global disaster risk analysis provides a basis for identifying situations in which future emergency recovery loans are likely to be needed. This creates an opportunity for "preappraising" emergency loans, that is, designing a risk management strategy to guide the allocation of emergency reconstruction resources should such resources become necessary, or to arrange for other types of contingency financing with development banks.

Improved Information for Disaster Risk Management

The Hotspots project provides a common framework for improving risk identification and promoting risk management through a dialogue between organizations and individuals operating at various geographic scales. The methods and results provide useful tools for integrating disaster risk management into development efforts and should be developed further.

As a global analysis conducted with very limited local-level participation and based on incomplete data, the results presented here should not provide the sole basis for designing risk management activities. The analysis does, however, provide a scientific basis for understanding where risks are highest and why, as well as a methodological framework for regional- and local-scale analysis. The identified risks then can be evaluated further using more detailed data in the context of a region's or country's overall development strategy and priorities.

We have designed the Hotspots approach to be open-ended to allow additional studies to be incorporated on an ongoing basis. It provides a common framework for improving risk identification and promoting risk management through a dialogue between organizations and individuals operating at various geographic scales. The Hotspots analysis can be improved upon as a tool and developed in several directions.

Improve Underlying Databases. The first direction is to pursue the many opportunities in both the short and long term to improve the underlying databases for assessing disaster risks and losses. A range of new global-scale data sets is currently under development, including a new global urban-extent database being developed by CIESIN in support of the Millennium Ecosystem Assessment. A joint project between the Earth Institute, the World Bank, and the Millennium Project will develop a much more detailed and complete database on subnational poverty and hunger. Much more comprehensive regional data sets will become available in specific areas of interest. On a regional scale, there are also much longer records of hazard events for specific hazards that could be harnessed to improve estimates of hazard frequency and intensity in high-risk areas (for example, O'Loughlin and Lander 2003). Significant improvements could be made in characterizing flood, drought and landslide hazards in particular. Existing data on disaster-related losses is being compiled into a multi-tiered system through which regularly updated historical data from multiple sources can be accessed. Additional work to link and cross-check existing data is needed, however, as is improvement in the assessment and documentation of global economic losses.

Undertake Case Studies. A second direction is to explore more fully the applicability and utility of the Hotspots approach to analysis and decision making at regional, national, and local scales. The initial case studies are promising, but are certainly not on their own sufficient to demonstrate the value of the overall approach or the specific data and methods under different conditions. More direct involvement of potential stakeholders would be valuable in extending the approach to finer scales of analysis and decision making. To be effective, efforts to improve risk identification in hotspot areas should be part of a complete package of technical and financial support for the full range of measures needed to manage disaster risks, including risk reduction and transfer.

Explore Long-term Trends. A third direction is to explore a key long-term issue: the potential effect of underlying changes in hazard frequency (for example, due to human-induced climatic change) coupled with long-term trends in human development and settlement patterns. To what degree could changes in tropical storm frequency, intensity, and position interact with continued coastal development (both urban and rural) to increase risks of death and destruction in these regions? Are agricultural areas, already under pressure from urbanization and other land use changes, likely to become more or less susceptible to drought, severe weather, or floods? Could other hazards such as wildfires potentially interact with changing patterns of drought, landslides, deforestation, and land use to create new types of hotspots? Although some aspects of these questions have been addressed in the general context of research on climate change impacts, the interactions between climate change, the full range of hazards, and evolving human hazard vulnerability have not been fully explored (for example, Brooks and Adger 2003; Chen 1994).

Pursuing work in these directions will necessarily involve a wide range of institutions—national, regional and international, public and private sector, academic and operational. We hope that the Hotspots project has contributed a building block in the foundation of a global effort to reduce disaster-related losses by managing risks rather than by managing emergencies. We look forward to continuing collaboration with partners at all levels to put in place a global disaster risk management support system in order to mobilize the knowledge and resources necessary to achieve this goal.

Chapter 2
Project Objectives

Hundreds of disasters occur worldwide each year in locations without sufficient local capacity or resources to prevent death and destruction and to support rapid recovery. Continuing rapid urbanization and coastal development in hazard-prone regions and the potential for long-term changes in the intensity and frequency of some hazards pose a serious challenge to sustainable development in both the developing and industrial worlds. Decision makers at all levels of governance, from the international to community levels, will face difficult choices about priorities for mitigating the risks of, for example, frequent, smaller hazards such as floods and landslides versus the risks of less frequent, more uncertain, but potentially much more deadly hazards such as earthquakes and tsunamis.

Natural disasters occur when large numbers of people or economic assets are damaged or destroyed during a natural hazard event. Disasters have two sets of causes. The first set is the natural hazards themselves, including floods, drought, tropical storms, earthquakes, volcanoes, and landslides. The second set comprises the vulnerabilities of elements at risk—populations, infrastructure, and economic activities—that make them more or less susceptible to being harmed or damaged by a hazard event.

Disaster-prone countries can be identified readily from existing databases of past disasters. Countries themselves may be aware of disaster-prone areas, either through local knowledge and experience or through formal risk assessments and historical data. The role of vulnerability as a causal factor in disaster losses tends to be less well understood, however. The idea that disasters can be managed by identifying and managing specific risk factors is only recently becoming widely recognized.

For the most part, both scientists and decision makers tend to deal with different hazards separately. For example, seismologists, structural engineers, and urban planners typically focus on mitigating earthquake risks through such efforts as strengthening building codes and structures, whereas climatologists, agronomists, and water resource managers address flood and drought risks through the development and maintenance of dams, reservoirs, and other water resource systems or through demand management. Although this approach is appropriate to some degree, given the differences in hazards and vulnerabilities, it is also important to consider and manage the *combined* risks of all hazards and vulnerabilities.

Disaster response is often handled by a variety of organizations at different levels of government and society, ranging from local volunteer groups to national civilian and military agencies to international relief agencies and nongovernmental organizations—each with its own areas of expertise with regard to particular disaster types and its own limitations in terms of jurisdiction and mode of operation. A more complete picture of multihazard risks can assist in developing coordinated strategies for total risk management.

The Hotspots project seeks to contribute to existing knowledge on global natural-disaster risks in the following ways:

1. Development of a spatially uniform, first-order, global disaster risk assessment through the use of global data sets in which the spatial distributions of hazards, elements at risk, and vulnerability factors, rather than national-level statistics, are the primary independent variables

2. Rigorous and precise definition of specific social and economic disaster-related outcomes, the risks of which can be quantitatively assessed globally

3. Identification of the hazard- and vulnerability-related causal components of risk on a hazard-by-hazard basis, taking into account the damaging characteristics of each hazard and the contingent vulnerability characteristics of potentially affected exposed elements

4. Assessment of overall, multihazard, global natural disaster risks, stated in terms of specific disaster outcomes (mortality and economic losses) for populations, infrastructure, and economic activities at risk

5. Verification of the global risk assessment through a limited number of case studies of limited geographic scope that allow risk factors to be characterized in greater detail through the use of larger scale data and involvement of national- to local-level stakeholders

6. Documentation of the hazard, vulnerability, and risk assessment methods used or generated in the analysis to extend the project's scope by enlisting others who wish to contribute to an ongoing, long-term, scientific effort to assess global risk

Disaster relief and recovery not only consume the lion's share of resources available for disaster management, but also drain resources away from other social and economic development priorities. Risk management investments in high-risk areas can be cost-effective in preventing disaster losses and increasing disaster preparation, leading to quicker, better planned recovery. Currently, high-risk areas typically are identified on the basis of national-level data of historical disasters and unevenly applied local knowledge. This project seeks to assess the geographic distribution of risks across national boundaries. Uniform data and methods provide comparability from one area to another.

Key stakeholders for the global analysis are international organizations that promote disaster risk management. For example, a global or regional lending organization might ask, *Where could a new lending program have the greatest risk reduction impact over the next 10 years? To what extent can existing data provide an adequate assessment of the degrees of hazard, exposure, vul-*

nerability, and risk? An international relief organization concerned with prepositioning disaster relief supplies might ask, *What hazards are likely to be of concern in areas inhabited by vulnerable populations? How can limited supplies be positioned optimally to address a range of possible hazard scenarios?*

In the long run, we also expect the Hotspots approach to be useful at the national and subnational levels. A national government might ask, *In areas that face risks from multiple hazards, which pose the most significant risks? What measures would be most effective in reducing vulnerability to all hazards? How much will achieving an acceptable level of risk cost, and how should resources be allocated?* A local government or community organization might ask, *Should certain risk management measures be avoided because they increase risks from other hazards? Can simple changes to development and mitigation plans result in long-term risk reduction? Is it possible to combine mitigation measures for single hazards cost-effectively?*

Both international institutions and the regions and countries they serve may seek a deeper understanding of potential barriers to disaster mitigation—not only technical and economic, but also cultural and political. They may wish to understand the long-term consequences of unmitigated disaster risk in terms of possible tradeoffs with long-term socioeconomic goals. *What are the opportunity costs and benefits of addressing disaster risk? How would overall wealth and the distribution of wealth be affected in the longer term? Could persistent impacts of disasters alter a country's global position in terms of future lending opportunities, trade, public health, or military security?*

There is growing recognition of the need for better data and information on hazards and disasters at both national and international levels. Within the United States, several recent reports by the U.S. National Research Council (NRC) and the U.S. government have highlighted the importance of both historical and current data on hazard events and their associated impacts (NRC 1999a, 1999b; Subcommittee on Disaster Reduction 2003). At the international level, there is strong interest in improving disaster information systems and associated decision support tools (for example, ISDR 2003).

A welcome shift in emphasis appears to be under way from managing disasters by managing emergencies to managing disaster risks. This shift is evident in recent publications such as the *2002 World Disasters Report:*

Focus on Reducing Risk (International Federation of Red Cross and Red Crescent Societies 2002), *Living with Risk* (ISDR 2004), *and Reducing Disaster Risk: A Challenge for Development* (UNDP 2004). Risk assessment, reduction, and transfer are the major elements of risk management (Kreimer and others 1999), offering a desirable alternative to managing disasters through emergency response. Risk reduction requires risk assessment in order to determine which areas are at highest risk of disaster and why, so that appropriate and cost-effective mitigation measures can be identified, adapted, and implemented.

As a global analysis conducted with very limited local-level participation and based on incomplete data, the results presented here should not provide the sole basis for designing risk management activities. The analysis does, however, provide a scientific basis for understanding where risks are highest and why, as well as a methodological framework for regional- and local-scale analysis. The identified risks then can be evaluated further using more detailed data in the context of a region's or country's overall development strategy and priorities.

We have designed the Hotspots approach to be open-ended to allow additional studies to be incorporated on an ongoing basis. It provides a common framework for improving risk identification and promoting risk management through a dialogue between organizations and individuals operating at various geographic scales.

Near-term applications of the analysis are expected to include the following:

1. A basis for further focus on high-risk areas by international institutions concerned with disaster risk management

2. Promotion of global/local partnerships for additional risk assessment and collaborative development and implementation of risk reduction plans in high-risk areas

3. Stimulation of further research on hazard and vulnerability risk factors in high-risk areas and on appropriate and cost-effective risk reduction and transfer measures

4. A model mode of analysis based on consistent disaster risk theory, assessment methods, and data that can be improved upon and applied globally and in particular locations

5. A platform of static risks over which dynamic risks can be overlaid at varying time scales, capturing seasonal-to-interannual fluctuations in hazard probabilities such as those associated with El Niño–Southern Oscillation (ENSO) events or long-term climatic trends, as well as socioeconomic risk factors and trends fluctuating on both short and long time scales

Chapter 3
Project Approach

A wide range of natural hazards cause death, damage, and other types of losses in both industrial and developing countries. Small-scale hazard events such as a small flood, tornado, landslide, lightning strike, or earth tremor may cause very localized damage, injuring or killing a few individuals and destroying or damaging a limited number of structures. In contrast, large-scale events such as hurricanes and tropical cyclones, strong earthquakes, large volcanic eruptions, tsunamis, major floods, and drought can kill tens of thousands of people and injure many more; they can also cause significant economic and social disruption as a result of both direct damage and indirect economic losses. Often large-scale events such as storms, earthquakes, and droughts spawn ancillary hazards such as floods, landslides, and wildfires that may add to casualties and economic losses. The severity of such secondary events may depend in part on environmental conditions such as soil moisture, land cover, and topography as well as on the presence and condition of protective works such as dams, dikes, and drainage systems.

Risk Assessment Framework

General Framework

In this project, we use the commonly accepted risk assessment framework for natural hazards (for example, Coburn and others 1994; Mileti 1999). In essence, we distinguish among three components that contribute to the overall risk of natural hazards:

1. The *probability of occurrence* of different kinds and intensities of hazards
2. The *elements exposed* to these hazards

3. The *vulnerability* of the elements exposed to specific hazards.

Disaster losses are caused by interactions between hazard events and the characteristics of exposed elements that make them susceptible to damage. A hazard's destructive potential is a function of the magnitude, duration, location, and timing of the event (Burton and others 1993). To be damaged, however, elements exposed to a given type of hazard must also be vulnerable to that hazard; that is, the elements must have intrinsic characteristics that allow them to be damaged or destroyed (UNDRO 1979). Valuable but vulnerable elements include people, infrastructure, and economically or environmentally important land uses.

The destructive power of natural hazards combined with vulnerabilities across a spectrum of exposed elements can lead to large-scale covariate losses during hazard events in areas where population and economic investment are concentrated. Aggregate losses start with losses to individual elements, reaching a point in disaster situations where economic and social systems break down partly or completely, leading to higher net socioeconomic impacts.

Risks of individual element losses or of aggregate covariate losses can be stated as the probability of loss, or as the proportion of elements that will be damaged or lost, over time (Coburn and others 1994). Disaster risk assessment examines the factors that cause losses in order to estimate loss probabilities. Risk factors include the probability of destructive hazard events as well as the contingent vulnerabilities of the exposed elements at risk.

The hazards research community has evolved a dynamic paradigm for hazards analysis that includes a four-stage process of hazard preparedness, response, recovery, and mitigation (Mileti 1999). Within this paradigm, assessment of vulnerability and risk is most useful at the stage of assessing hazard preparedness and designing hazard mitigation strategies. Indeed, Mileti and colleagues have recommended adoption of a "global systems perspective" that recognizes the complex "interactions between earth and social systems, within and across the global-to-local levels of human aggregation" (Mileti 1999: 27). The Hotspots approach is consistent with this perspective.

Terminology

In its simplest terms, we define a natural disaster "hotspot" as a *specific area or region that may be at relatively high risk of adverse impacts from one or more natural hazard events.* Use of the term "adverse" implies a normative judgment that at least some of the major consequences of a hazardous event are considered undesirable by those affected: for example, the death or injury of people, damage to, or loss of, economically valuable assets, or lost income and employment. Impacts on natural ecosystems may also be of concern but are not explicitly addressed in this project. However, it is important to recognize that, for example, tropical storms may have adverse impacts on coastal populations in their immediate path but beneficial effects on agriculture and water resources over much larger areas. The focus of disaster management is to reduce or ameliorate the adverse impacts, generally in the context of other societal efforts to take advantage of beneficial effects.

Given the variety of natural hazards that continue to cause significant adverse impacts in both industrial and developing countries, we categorize hotspots into two major types:

1. *Single-hazard hotspots.* Some areas or regions may be at relatively high risk of adverse impacts associated with one major natural hazard. For example, seismologists have predicted that there is a 47–77 percent probability that the city of Istanbul, Turkey—with a population estimated at 8.7 million in 2000 (U.N. Population Division 2004)—will experience strong shaking during the first 30 years of this century, with great potential for death, injury, damage, and economic disruption (Hubert-Ferrari and others 2000; Parsons and others 2000).

2. *Multihazard hotspots.* Some areas may be subject to a variety of natural hazards and associated moderate to high levels of risk of loss. In some cases, the hazards themselves may be largely independent of each other; that is, the occurrence of one hazard does not significantly affect the probability that other hazards will occur. However, even if this is the case, the occurrence of one hazard might significantly affect the overall impacts of other hazards. For example, after a major tsunami hit Papua New Guinea (PNG) in July 1998, the PNG embassy issued an appeal in which it noted, "The tsunami is the latest of a series of natural disasters striking Papua New Guinea in the last three and a half years. The volcano eruption in Rabaul, cyclone Justin's destruction in the Milne Bay area, and the El Niño-induced drought in most parts of the country, have caused a horrendous burden on the Government and the people of Papua New Guinea" (*International Disaster Situation Reports,* 23 July 1998; see http://www.cidi.org/disaster/98b/0021.html).

For both types of hotspot, exposure and vulnerability must be high before risks are considered significant. Such exposure and vulnerability could be in the form of important economic assets, such as agricultural areas that are vulnerable to drought or flood hazards. In areas of relatively low population density, some hazards could still pose high mortality (and morbidity) risks if vulnerability is high because of fragile infrastructure or other factors. In very high-density areas, even low vulnerability (low casualty rates) could result in substantial losses in absolute terms (many deaths), especially among those who may have higher-than-average vulnerability (for example, slum dwellers living on steep slopes).

Throughout this report, we use the term *hazard* to represent a specific family of natural phenomena and *degree of hazard* to signify a particular hazard-dependent measure of severity. *Exposure* represents the overlap of time and spatial distribution of human assets and the time and spatial distribution of hazard events. We use the term *vulnerability* to represent the apparent weaknesses of physical and social systems to particular hazards. Physical system vulnerability is usually defined (especially in the engineering community) in terms of *fragility curves,* in which the weaknesses of physical systems (buildings and infrastructure, for example) are quantified as a function of hazard severity. Similar fragility curves for social systems—that is, a quantification of social vulnerability—are complex functions of social, economic, political, and cultural variables and are addressed in this report through the use of proxies. In general terms, *risk* is a multiplicative function of hazard severity, exposure, and fragility.

Limitations and Uncertainty

In designing the methodology for this report, we have been forced to accommodate the inherent heterogeneity that characterizes risk assessments across multiple natural hazards. Although some attempts have been made (most notably by the insurance industry) to develop common risk metrics (such as average annualized loss: see Risk Management Solutions 2004), such methods are themselves based on highly variable data quality, incomplete fragility analysis, and insufficient historical records. Where such data and analysis exist, as they do for some regions, more comprehensive risk assessment is possible (as we point out in the case studies).

Our goal in this report is to estimate the relative multihazard risk countries face using defensible measures of degree of hazard and defensible proxies for physical and social vulnerabilities. Our metrics for degree of hazard or hazard severity vary according to the hazard. In our view, the science of hazard occurrence and magnitude has not developed enough to permit a globally consistent single metric for multihazard severity. Such metrics are currently the subject of basic research programs. Lacking widely applicable measures of physical fragility and social vulnerability, and lacking even uniform standards for collecting the loss data needed to calibrate fragility, we have chosen to use broadly accepted and relatively uniform proxies for vulnerability in the form of masked population density, GDP, and transportation network density, as normalized by total losses in the Emergency Events Database (EM-DAT). As we explain in the next section, we use a geographic mask designed to identify agricultural land use and high population density as first-order selection criteria to quantify the geographic distribution of exposure.

An analysis of this sort is not amenable to a quantitative estimation of either aleatoric or epistemic uncertainties. A meaningful error analysis may not be possible given the state of knowledge about hazard occurrence,

fragility, and loss, especially in the time frames required for policy decisions and mitigation investments. Instead, we propose that this analysis be a basis for developing scenarios and counter-factual analyses of mitigation alternatives to give policymakers a framework for their investment decisions. The role of uncertainties can be included in such scenarios, as they relate to decision support, but the actual degrees of uncertainty are unlikely to be useful in the near future. However, this lack of certainty should not be taken as an excuse for inaction.

Selection of Natural Hazards

Data on natural hazards have been collected by different groups for different purposes in different ways. The most comprehensive, publicly available global database on natural hazards and their impacts is the EM-DAT data set maintained by the Centre for Research on the Epidemiology of Disasters (CRED) in Brussels (Sapir and Misson 1992; see www.cred.be). This database contains more than 12,000 records of disasters from 1900 to the present, compiled from multiple sources. It includes estimates of numbers of people killed and affected as well as estimates of economic losses, derived from documented sources. In many cases, these loss estimates include direct losses not only from the primary event (for example, a cyclone or earthquake) but also from subsequent related events such as landslides and floods. The database generally does not include geophysical or hydro-meteorological events that were not reported as causing heavy losses, either because the events occurred in areas that were thinly populated at the time, or because the losses were not reported in English- or French-language periodicals.

In addition to the EM-DAT database, this project has taken advantage of data sets developed by different groups around the world focused on specific hazard probabilities, occurrences, or extents. This approach has permitted us to identify areas that will be at relatively high risk of particular types of hazard events in the future, regardless of their past levels of exposure or actual losses. Our approach assumes that existing databases are more likely to underreport smaller events than large events. Areas at higher risk from large events therefore probably will be more accurately identified than areas that suffer from smaller, more frequent events. However, the short record periods for some large but infrequent hazard events (for example, volcanic eruptions) suggest that efforts to assess absolute levels of risk or to compare risk levels across hazards would be premature.

Table 3.1 lists the major natural hazards reported in EM-DAT, ranked by the total number of deaths reported. For this analysis, we selected six major disaster types for analysis: drought, tropical storms, floods, earthquakes, volcanoes, and landslides. We did not attempt to assess extreme temperature events (heat and cold waves), wildfires, and wave/surge events such as tsunamis, owing to data and resource limitations. Nor did we assess some hazards that are primarily of regional or economic concern, such as tornadoes, hail, and lightning. However, in principle these hazards could be included in future efforts to improve and expand the hotspots approach.

Units of Analysis

Most efforts to assess the impacts of natural hazards have used either events or countries as the basic unit of analysis. That is, they have examined known occurrences of hazards and associated impacts either on an event-by-event basis or as aggregated to the national level.

This project takes advantage of new methods and data that make possible a more detailed geospatial analysis across multiple hazards. Although hazard mapping efforts began in the 1970s (for example, White and Haas

1975), these efforts were severely constrained by the lack of detailed data, especially at the global level, as well as by limitations in computational capabilities and data integration methods.

In 1994–95, the first global-scale gridded population data set, known as the Gridded Population of the World (GPW), version 1 data set, was developed with primary support from CIESIN (Tobler and others 1995). This data set transformed population census data, which most countries collected for subnational administrative units, into a regular "grid" of "spherical quadrilaterals" with the dimensions of 5 minutes (5') of latitude and 5 minutes (5') of longitude and an average area of about 55 square kilometers each (85 square kilometers at the equator). Each cell contained an estimate of total population and population density (on land) for 1994, based on the overlap between the irregular boundaries of the administrative units and the regular boundaries of the grid. Version 2 of GPW was developed by CIESIN in collaboration with the International Food Policy Research Institute (IFPRI) and the World Resources Institute (WRI). Its cells have a nominal resolution of 2.5' latitude by 2.5' longitude and contain population estimates for 1990 and 1995 (CIESIN and others 2000). A beta test version of Version 3 is currently available with population estimates for 1990, 1995, and 2000 with the same nominal resolution as GPW Version 2 (CIESIN and others 2004). With each new version, the number of subnational administrative units used to create these gridded population estimates has increased, from about 19,000 units in Version 1 to 127,000 in Version 2 to about 375,000 in Version 3. The underlying detail of the spatial distributions has therefore increased dramatically. The improvement in resolution is summarized in Table 3.2.

Using the 2.5' x 2.5' grid as a base, it is possible to make a variety of estimates of hazard probability, occurrence, and extent on a common geospatial frame of reference. It is also possible to add supplementary measures of exposure such as the density of roads and railroads, the amount of agricultural land, and the economic value-added to the same framework. The result is a grid of approximately 8.7 million cells covering most of the occupied land area of the Earth within latitudes 85°N to 58°S. Each grid cell contains estimates of land area, population, population density, various hazard proba-

Table 3.1. Ranking of Major Natural Hazards by Number of Deaths Reported in EM-DAT

Rank	Disaster Type	All Deaths 1980–2000*	Deaths 1992–2001**
1	Drought	563,701	277,574
2	Storms	251,384	60,447
3	Floods	170,010	96,507
4	Earthquakes	158,551	77,756
5	Volcanoes	25,050	259
6	Extreme temperature	19,249	10,130
7	Landslides	18,200	9,461
8	Wave/surge	3,068	2,708
9	Wildfires	1,046	574
	Total	1,211,159	535,416

* Compiled by O. Kjekstad, personal communication
** 2002 IFRC World Disaster Report (http://www.cred.be/emdat/intro.htm)

Table 3.2. Number of Input Units Used in the Gridded Population of the World (GPW) Data Sets, Versions 1–3

Version	Year Released	Estimates for	Input Units
GPW v1	1995	1994	19,000
GPW v2	2000	1990, 1995	127,000
GPW v3	2003/04	1990, 1995, 2000	~ 375,000

bilities, and associated exposure and vulnerability characteristics. These grid cells may be aggregated, either to a larger grid (for example, a 1° x 1° latitude/longitude grid) or to national boundaries (making simple assumptions about grid cells along borders).

Since the objective of this analysis is to identify hotspots where natural hazard impacts may be large, it need not include the large proportion of the Earth's surface that is sparsely populated and not intensively used. We have therefore chosen to mask out grid cells with population densities less than five persons per square kilometer (cells with less than about 105 residents) and without significant agriculture. Even if all residents of such cells were exposed and highly vulnerable to a hazard, total casualties would still be relatively small in absolute terms, and the potential agricultural impact would be limited.[1]

Masking these cells reduces data processing requirements and ensures that the large number of very low risk cells do not dominate the results. In addition, hazard reporting and frequency data are likely to be poorest in rural, sparsely populated areas, so masking could reduce anomalies caused by poor data. A total of approximately 4.1 million grid cells remain after applying the mask (Figure 3.1). These cells (colored orange, blue, or green in the figure) include slightly more than half of the world's estimated land area (about 72 million square kilometers, or about 55 percent of the total), but most of the world's population (6 billion people, or about 99.2 percent of the population estimate in GPW for the year 2000).

Summary of Data Sources and Data Preparation

Hazard Data

The first step in the hotspots analysis was to examine each hazard individually in terms of available spatial data on probability, occurrence, or extent. The most desirable input data would be complete probability density functions for each hazard, that is, the probabilities of occurrence of a specific hazard for a range of severities or intensities in a specific future time period. Unfortunately, detailed probabilistic data of this type do not exist for any hazards at the global level. A more limited probabilistic estimate is available for earthquakes: the Global Seismic Hazard Program (GSHAP) has used both historic data and expert judgment to derive a global map of the peak ground acceleration (pga) for which there is a 10 percent chance of exceedance in the next 50 years.

Even without detailed probabilistic data, however, it is still possible to distinguish between areas of higher and lower risk using occurrence data, that is, data on specific events that took place during a given historical period. The area affected by the events must be determined by analysis or modeling of available data.

The data identified and used for each hazard are summarized in Table 3.3. More detailed descriptions of the individual data sets acquired and the transformations applied are given in Appendix A.1. A brief summary for each hazard follows:

1. *Cyclones.* For cyclones, we used storm track data collected from multiple sources and assembled into geographic information system (GIS) coverages by the UNEP/GRID (Global and Regional Integrated Data)-Geneva Project of Risk Evaluation, Vulnerability, Information and Early Warning (PreView). This data set includes more than 1,600 storm tracks for the period 1 January 1980 through 31 December 2000 for the Atlantic, Pacific, and Indian Oceans.[2] As described in detail in Appendix A.1, we modeled the wind speeds around the storm tracks in order to assess the grid cells likely to have been exposed to high wind levels.

---

[1] To determine agricultural land use, we used the U.S. Geological Survey (USGS) Global Land Cover Classification database at 30″ resolution and dropped from the mask any cells with any one of three land covers typically associated with agriculture (Sebastian, personal communication, 2003). If any of the 25 30″ cells in a 2.5′ cell included an agricultural land cover, we dropped the entire 2.5′ cell from the mask.

[2] The record for the 1980s for some parts of the Indian and Pacific Oceans are incomplete in some cases. See: http://www.grid.unep.ch/data/grid/gnv199.php.

Figure 3.1. Mask Used to Eliminate Sparsely Populated, Nonagricultural Areas

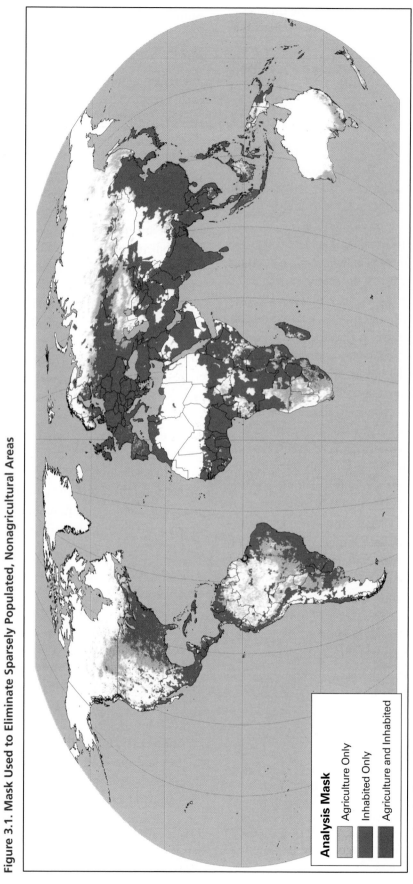

Analysis Mask

Agriculture Only

Inhabited Only

Agriculture and Inhabited

Note: Colored cells are those retained.

2. *Drought*. For drought, we used the Weighted Anomaly of Standardized Precipitation (WASP) developed by IRI, computed on a 2.5° x 2.5° grid from monthly average precipitation data for 1980 through 2000. The WASP assesses the precipitation deficit or surplus over a specified number of months, weighted by the magnitude of the seasonal cyclic variation in precipitation. A three-month running average was applied to the precipitation data and the median rainfall for the 21-year period calculated for each grid point. A mask was applied to eliminate grid points where the three-month running average precipitation was less than 1 millimeter per day. This excluded both desert regions and dry seasons from the analysis. For the remaining points, a drought event was identified when the magnitude of a monthly precipitation deficit was less than or equal to 50 percent of its long-term median value for three or more consecutive months.

3. *Floods*. The Dartmouth Flood Observatory has compiled a global listing of extreme flood events from diverse sources and georeferenced to the nearest degree for 1985 through 2003. Flood extent data are based on regions affected by floods, not necessarily on flooded areas. Data are poor or missing in the early-mid 1990s.

4. *Earthquakes*. For earthquakes, we used both the GSHAP data and a database of actual earthquake events greater than 4.5 on the Richter scale for 1976 through 2002 (Advanced National Seismic System 1997). The GSHAP data were sampled at 1' intervals, with a minimum peak ground acceleration of 2 meters per second per second (m/s^2), or approximately one-fifth of surface gravitational acceleration.

5. *Volcanoes*. For volcanoes, we used a spatial coverage of volcanic activity (79 A.D. through 2000 A.D.) developed by UNEP-GRID Geneva based on the Worldwide Volcano Database and available at the National Geophysical Data Center (http://www.ngdc.noaa.gov/seg/hazard/vol_srch.shtml). This database includes nearly 4,000 events categorized as moderate or above (values 2–8) according to the Volcano Explosivity Index (VEI) developed by Simkin and Seibert (1994). Some volcanoes are located to the nearest thousandth of a degree, but most have been georeferenced to the nearest tenth or hundredth of a degree.

6. *Landslides*. The NGI, working with UNEP GRID-Geneva and this project, has developed a global landslide and snow avalanche hazard map that has been used for global analysis of these hazards. The map is based on a range of data including slope, soil and soil moisture conditions, precipitation, seismicity, and temperature (NGI 2004). This index takes advantage of more detailed elevation data that recently became available from the Shuttle Radar Topographic Mission (SRTM) at 30" resolution, compiled and corrected by Isciences, L.L.C. (http://www.isciences.com).

Table 3.3. Summary of Data Sources for Each Hazard

Hazard	Parameter	Period	Resolution	Source(s)
Cyclones	Frequency by wind strength	1980–2000	30"	UNEP/GRID-Geneva PreView
Drought	Weighted Anomaly of Standardized Precipitation (50% below normal precip. for a 3-month period)	1980–2000	2.5°	IRI Climate Data Library
Floods	Counts of extreme flood events	1985–2003*	1°	Dartmouth Flood Observatory, World Atlas of Large Flood Events
Earthquakes	Expected pga > 2 m/s^2 (10% probability of exceedance in 50 years)	n/a	sampled at 1'	Global Seismic Hazard Program
	Frequency of earthquakes > 4.5 on Richter Scale	1976–2002	sampled at 2.5'	Advanced National Seismic System Earthquake Catalog
Volcanoes	Counts of volcanic activity	79–2000	Sampled at 2.5'	UNEP/GRID-Geneva and NGDC
Landslides	Index of landslide and snow avalanche hazard	n/a	30"	NGI

*Missing data for 1989, 1992, 1996, and 1997; quality of spatial data for 1990–91 and 1993–95 limited.
n/a = not available.

Selection of Severity Metrics

As we assert above, globally uniform data do not yet exist to produce a justifiable measure of hazard severity that can be applied consistently across multiple hazards. Instead we have chosen to use severity metrics appropriate for each of the hazards studied in this report. This necessarily introduces a degree of heterogeneity in our analysis. But at this stage in natural hazard studies, it is more important to develop a homogeneous representation of normalized loss and risk, which we have attempted to do through the use of well-accepted proxies. We argue that the choice of different hazard severity metrics for different hazards should be informed by the known relative losses for historical events, so that we can achieve relative parity in the treatment of multiple hazards on an expected loss and geographical basis. Such an approach would tend to underemphasize extreme events, that is, infrequent or unexpected high-impact events. (The question remains how extreme events should be treated in a global relative analysis. By definition, their occurrences are highly uncertain and their impacts highly specific. However, singular events may dominate a country's total loss profile. This is an area for further research.)

Earthquakes

We rely on the exceedance probabilities presented in the GSHAP maps. This calculation uses the empirical space-time distribution of earthquake occurrence to develop a probabilistic estimate of maximum ground shaking at each grid point. To use these maps in our analysis, we must therefore choose both a lower cutoff for shaking amplitude (ground acceleration) and a characteristic repeat time for that cutoff to be achieved. We have chosen to use a relatively short repeat time (chance of exceeding lower ground motion cutoff is 10 percent in 50 years, or once in 500 years) in order to emphasize more common events and repetitive disasters. This deemphasizes rare extreme events, but losses from such events are not well calibrated and thus have relatively little predictive value. At the same time, basic research into the occurrence of such large events is continuing; such research holds the promise that the occurrence of large earthquakes will be better understood in the near future.

We also choose a lower cutoff of 2 m/s² for ground acceleration. The choice of cutoff determines to a large extent (for fixed repeat time) the geographic overlap with assets, based on the GSHAP calculation alone. However, the geographic area susceptible to destructive ground shaking from a particular event is also affected by such unmodeled variables as soil quality, attenuation of earthquake energy in the earth's crust, and pathological characteristics of the earthquake source itself. Although weak buildings can be damaged severely by ground shaking as low as 1 m/s² (or even lower), the uncertainties associated with these other factors render arguments over the lower cutoff moot. Instead, we have chosen the cutoff to represent subjectively the major attributes of the spatial distribution of damaging earthquakes, namely, that the most significant damage occurs near the known geologic expression of active tectonic boundaries. Some events, such as the Mexico City earthquake in 1985, have pathological damage distribution patterns and are not well modeled by this choice. On the other hand, the choice of a lower cutoff would enlarge the geographic overlap to such an extent that comparisons with other hazards would be vitiated and unrealistic.

We emphasize this last point by showing actual earthquake locations (seismicity) as well as the pga maps. This is somewhat redundant, as the GSHAP calculation uses essentially the same data. However, the seismicity maps support the choice of lower pga cutoff.

Drought

The definition of drought hazard events as rainfall at 50 percent or less of the median for three months was based on a number of factors. A modified version of this definition was found to maximize the correlation between drought hazard events and EM-DAT mortality in a companion study (UNDP 2004). In the semiarid tropics, where drought-related risks are highest, three- to four-month rainfall seasons are typical. Rainfall at 50 percent or less of the median for three months therefore poses a significant threat. Finally, experimentation with various cutoffs—longer or shorter periods or alternative percentages of the median—resulted in spatial patterns in which droughts were either too pervasive or too insignificant to explain observed losses. Although the resulting definition produces a spatial pattern of drought frequency that is not totally satisfactory in all regions, it was judged the best overall. The IRI and CRED are currently designing a study to systematically examine climate-loss relationships over 800 historical drought disasters to arrive at a more rigorous drought hazard definition.

Exposure Data

To understand the risks posed by a range of hazards, it is also essential to characterize the exposure of people and their economic activities to the different hazards. Ideally, we would have a complete probability density function for population exposure to specific types of events; that is, we would know the probabilities that particular populations for a range of event sizes and characteristics would be present in the grid cells directly affected by those events. Such estimates might vary depending on the time of day, day of week, or month of the year, as well as on local holiday schedules, given that individuals in many industrial and developing countries may travel across multiple grid cells in the course of a day, week, or month. For longer term events such as drought, a time-averaged population estimate or an estimate of population involved in agriculture might be more appropriate for assessing exposure.

For this initial, global-scale analysis, however, we believe that a consistent population estimate based on reported residence is appropriate to characterize population exposure across different hazard types. We use an estimate of population for the year 2000, developed as part of GPW Version 3, to characterize the "current" distribution of population. Although population distribution is likely to change in the future because of differential rates of population change, including urban and coastal migration and different fertility and mor-

tality rates, we have little basis for projecting these changes into the future (Gaffin and others 2004).

To capture the hazard exposure of human economic infrastructure and activity, it would be ideal to have detailed measures of the extent and quality of infrastructure and the economic value of the exposed land and resources. Unfortunately, consistent, spatially disaggregated data on these parameters are very limited. In the United States, for example, although most local jurisdictions assess property values for the purpose of tax assessment, the ratio between actual market values and assessed values varies greatly. Detailed sample surveys of this ratio were conducted at the county level in the early 1970s but were later discontinued (Schneider and Chen 1980). We have also explored whether satellite remote sensing data could be used to assess infrastructure consistently around the world, but the available techniques and data at this point appear insufficient (Nghiem and others 2002).

We have therefore chosen to use several crude measures of economic activity and infrastructure on an exploratory basis (Table 3.4). More detailed descriptions of the methods and data sources are provided in Appendix A.1.

The total level of economic activity at the national level is measured by the GDP, the annual market value of final goods and services produced by a country. For about 50 countries, more than half of which are developing or transitional economies (including Bangladesh, Brazil, China, India, Indonesia, and Mexico), GDP data are available for subnational units. Following Sachs and coauthors (2001), we applied these subnational estimates to population density, using the World Bank estimates of GDP based on purchasing power parity (PPP) for 2000.

Table 3.4. Summary of Data Sources for Exposure

Exposure	Parameter	Period	Resolution	Source(s)
Land	Land area	2000	2.5"	GPW Version 3 (beta)
Population	Population counts/density	2000	2.5"	GPW Version 3 (beta)
Economic Activity	National/subnational GDP	2000	2.5"	World Bank DECRG based on Sachs and others (2001)
Agricultural Activity	National agricultural GDP allocated to agricultural land area	2000	2.5"	World Bank DECRG based on Sachs and others (2001)
Road Density	Length of major roads and railroads	c. 1993	2.5"	VMAP(0)

To provide an exposure measure relevant to floods and drought, we allocated available national estimates of agricultural GDP to grid cells based on the amount of agricultural land. This assumes, very crudely, that all agricultural areas contribute equally to the total agricultural GDP for the country.

Finally, as a measure of infrastructure development, we computed the total length of major roads and railroads for each grid cell based on the VMAP(0) data sets developed by the National Geospatial-Intelligence Agency (formerly the National Imagery and Mapping Agency) and made available by the USGS (http://erg.usgs.gov/nimamaps/dodnima.html#Digital).

We recognize that these measures provide at best only first-order indicators of the level of exposure and, given the lack of detailed spatial data, may significantly under- or overstate exposure in any particular grid cell. However, we believe that these indicators may be useful in broadly classifying different levels of exposure in order to better characterize the relative risks associated with different hazards. A summary of the totals of each measure for the world and the area retained after applying the mask is provided in Table 3.5.

Vulnerability Data

The stresses to which a given element at risk is subjected during a hazard event depend on the hazard. These stresses include shaking in the case of earthquakes, moisture stress in the case of drought, inundation during floods, and so on. A given element may be severely challenged by one hazard but completely unaffected by another. A building, for example, may collapse when subjected to seismic shaking or incur damage due to floods, but may suffer little or no impact during a drought. Similarly, the fertility of agricultural land may benefit directly as a result of flooding, whereas exposed infrastructure may be severely damaged.

For a given hazard, vulnerability will vary across similar elements and from one element to the next. Irrigated agricultural areas tend to experience lower losses during droughts than areas that depend on rainfall, for example. Buildings that are constructed to seismic safety standards are less likely to be damaged during an earthquake than those built of unreinforced masonry. Houses with raised platforms are better suited to withstanding flood conditions that those without. People and societies with resources and economic alternatives tend to be better protected from harm and able to recover more quickly than people with fewer options and resources.

The set of elements that may be damaged by a given hazard is often quite large. Urban infrastructure, for example, consists of multiple sectors—transport, power, water and sanitation, housing, and communications—each of which in turn may encompass many separate systems. Each system is made of subsystems and so on, down to the level of individual components.

When a complex entity such as an urban area is subjected to a severe hazard event like a flood or volcanic eruption, widespread failures of vulnerable components can cause total or partial system failure, resulting in a disaster. Given the number of systems, subsystems, and components, each of which responds differently when subjected to a given hazard, it is possible to characterize vulnerability only generally (or perhaps stochastically) when operating at scales larger than individual installations or facilities. Similarly, when social systems such as communities or households are the unit of analysis, vulnerability analysis requires detailed knowledge of household or community characteristics. In a global analysis such as the current one, therefore, vulnerability assessment is at best possible only through the use of general proxies.

This analysis assesses global disaster-related risks of mortality and economic losses. The elements at risk are

Table 3.5. Summary of Exposure Data for World and Unmasked Areas

	*Total**	*Within Mask*	*Percentage Within Mask*
Land Area (million km²)	131	72	54.9
Population 2000 (millions)	6,054	6,008	99.2
GDP (PPP, billion US$, 2000)	44,198	43,544	98.5
Agricultural Value (billion US$, 2000)	1,361	1,359	99.8
Transportation (million km)	7.9	6.4	80.8

* All grid cells within GPW, Version 3 (beta).

people in the first instance and an estimated value of goods and services produced annually per unit area in the second. Ideally, we would have a complete probability density function for the loss expected to result when particular populations or economic assets are exposed to a range of hazards and hazard severities (that is, we would know the probabilities of different levels of losses likely to be experienced by the exposed units in the grid cells directly affected by different hazard events). Owing to data limitations, we used historical loss rates, using a methodology described in detail below. We calculated loss rates for each hazard from historical losses over 20 years (1981 through 2000) obtained from EM-DAT. For each hazard we calculated 28 loss rates, one for each combination of seven regions and four country wealth status groups based on World Bank classifications.

Estimates of losses per disaster and the degree to which disaster events are consistently captured vary from one data source to the next (Sapir and Misson 1992). For the purpose of estimating loss rates, however, it is not necessary to assume that EM-DAT contains a complete inventory of all deaths and economic losses over the 20-year period. Rather, in this analysis, it is only necessary that the deaths and economic damages recorded in EM-DAT capture *relative* differences in mortality and economic losses between hazards, regions, and country wealth groupings. Improvements in mortality and economic loss data by event in data sets such as EM-DAT would make loss rate calculation more precise. For example, the insurance industry has been developing more consistent loss databases for selected regions and in at least one case has developed a multihazard index of average annual loss based on modeled exposure to hazard events (Risk Management Solutions 2004).

Global Hotspots Classification

Classification of hotspots on a global basis addresses the central concern of the project—the identification and characterization of high-risk natural disaster hotspots. Because of the limited time period and quality of the input data, we believe that it is appropriate to use the data to identify areas at *relatively* high risk of a particular natural hazard, and then to compare the spatial dis-

tributions of the resulting hazard maps. The data may be inadequate for assessing absolute risk levels or for detailed comparisons of risk levels across hazards. For a number of the available hazard data sets, such as those based on media reports, we also expect that relatively small or modest events may be undercounted substantially, especially in developing countries where reporting is likely to be less complete.

We therefore divided the total number of grid cells into *deciles*, ten groups of approximately equal number of cells, based on the value of each individual hazard indicator. Cells with the value of zero for an indicator were excluded. When hazard indicators have large numbers of cells with the same values (cyclones, drought, floods, and earthquakes), deciles may be grouped together. For example, the result of dividing the flood data into deciles results in output values of 1, 4, and 7 through 10. Since many grid cells have only one or two flood events, the first through third deciles are combined and given the output value 1, and the fourth through sixth deciles are combined and given the output value 4. In all cases, the combined deciles are at the low end of the scale (sixth decile or less).

Results for each hazard are discussed in detail in Section 4. In general, at least the top three deciles of cells were needed to identify areas of known hazard around the world. As an initial arbitrary cutoff, we therefore chose the top three deciles as our first-order definition of "relative significance" in terms of hazard frequency or probability, exposure, and overall risk. Some cells are classified as relatively high in significance according to more than one hazard, that is, they fall within the top three deciles of more than one hazard indicator. We therefore built an index that simply sums the decile values for each hazard, with 8 representing the third highest decile, 9 representing the second highest decile, and 10 the highest decile. Thus, a cell in the third decile for just one hazard would have an index value of 8, and a cell in the third highest decile for just two hazards would have an index value of 16. A cell in the top three deciles for three hazards would have an index value between 24 and 30. Results are presented in Chapter 5.

Using the same cutoff of the top three deciles for each natural hazard identifies those cells that are at higher relative probability compared with other cells for each *hazard,* but does not necessarily result in comparable levels of *absolute* probability across hazards. That is, a cell in the top three deciles for both flood and drought hazards does not necessarily face the same probability of hazard occurrence in terms of drought and flood frequency and intensity. Moreover, hazards such as floods, earthquakes, and volcanoes have very different patterns of occurrence in terms of their spatial distributions, temporal recurrence, and event characteristics, making absolute comparisons difficult. Given the very limited records available at the global scale, we think that it is currently impossible to determine compara-

ble absolute levels of probability. Moreover, the potential exposure of land, population, and other features of each cell varies greatly both across cells and over time, so that the overall level of risk faced in a multihazard hotspot will be determined by a range of highly uncertain factors.

We have experimented with alternative approaches to index construction, weighting the decile values by measures of exposure, population density, and GDP density, and then by regional measures of vulnerability. We present and compare these results in Chapters 5 and 6.

Chapter 4
Single-Hazard Exposure Analysis

Figures 4.1a–g presents hazard maps for the six natural hazards, including two different indicators of earthquake hazard. All of these figures are based on deciles, with the top three deciles indicated in red, the next three deciles in yellow, and the bottom four deciles in blue. Areas with very low population and minimal agricultural production are masked as described in Chapter 3.

Cyclones

At least 6.7 percent of the world's land area was subject to at least one instance of high wind speeds associated with a tropical storm or cyclone during the 21-year period of record. Notably, these coastal areas are more densely populated than average, so that approximately 24 percent of the world's population, more than 1.4 billion people, lives in the affected areas. Similarly, GDP, agricultural production, and transportation infrastructure also appear more concentrated in these areas than average (33 percent, 19 percent, and 13 percent of total land area, respectively).

The top three deciles of grid cells (red areas of Figure 4.1a) include about 2.5 million square kilometers (1.9 percent) and more than 550 million residents (9.1 percent) (Table 4.1). GDP density is more than eight times greater than the world average; these exposed areas represent about one-sixth of total world GDP.

The most frequently hit areas are in the western Pacific, southern Africa, the Caribbean, and southeastern United States. Surprisingly, Bangladesh and neighboring areas do not show up in the highest deciles, even though they have been impacted significantly in the past by severe storm surge. This may be due to the somewhat more limited record of Indian Ocean storms. It also appears

that many of the storm tracks in the database do not actually reach land. Since our indicator is based only on wind speed and not on storm surge potential, it may underestimate the potential hazard.

Drought

Drought exhibits a more dispersed pattern around the globe, with 2.5° x 2.5° grid cells in the top three deciles (red areas of Figure 4.1b) appearing in both interior and coastal regions of most continents. These drought-prone areas include parts of the western and midwestern United States, Central America, northeastern Brazil, the sub-Saharan belt, the Horn of Africa, southern and central Africa, Madagascar, southern Spain and Portugal, central Asia, northwest India, northeast China, Southeast Asia, Indonesia, and southern Australia.

About 38 percent of the world's land area has some level of drought exposure. This 38 percent contains about 70 percent of both the total population and the agricultural value produced. In the top three deciles of drought-prone grid cells, about 1.1 billion people (18 percent) live in about 12.9 million square kilometers of land (10 percent). The highest decile alone contains about 419 million people because of a somewhat higher than average population density.

Floods

Some flooding is evident in more than one-third of the world's land area, in which some 82 percent of the world's population resides (red, green, and blue areas of Figure 4.1c). The most flood-prone areas (indicated in red) encompass about 9 percent of the land area and

35

Figure 4.1. Distribution of Hazardous Areas by Hazard Type
a) Cyclones

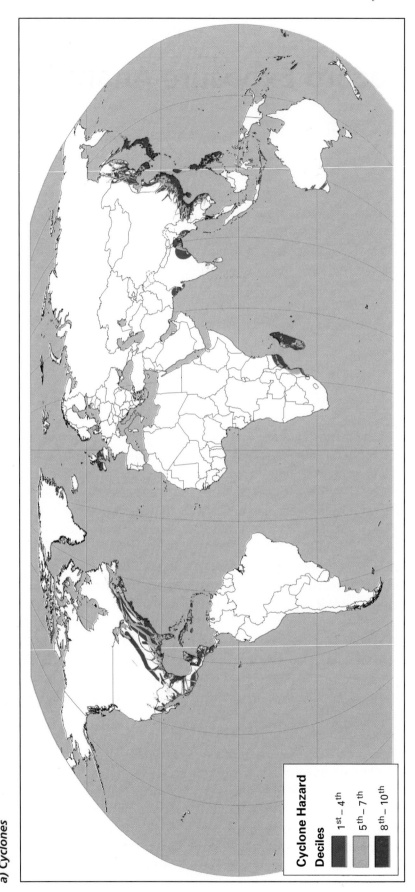

Cyclone Hazard
Deciles

1st – 4th
5th – 7th
8th – 10th

Figure 4.1. Distribution of Hazardous Areas by Hazard Type
b) Drought

Drought Hazard
Deciles

1st – 4th
5th – 7th
8th – 10th

Figure 4.1. Distribution of Hazardous Areas by Hazard Type
c) Floods

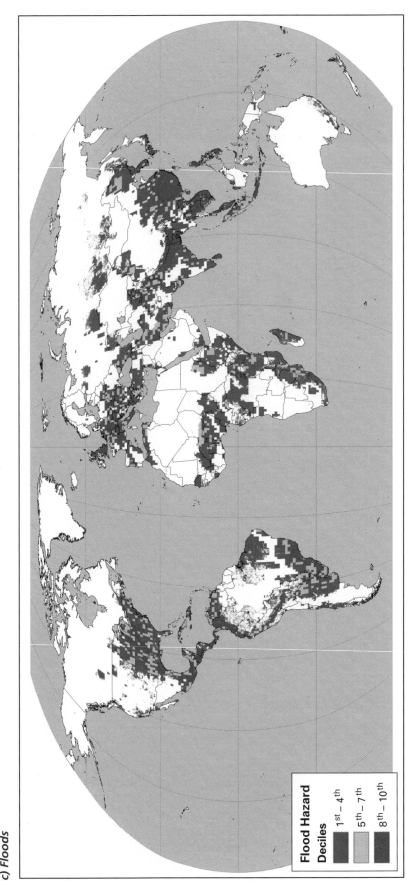

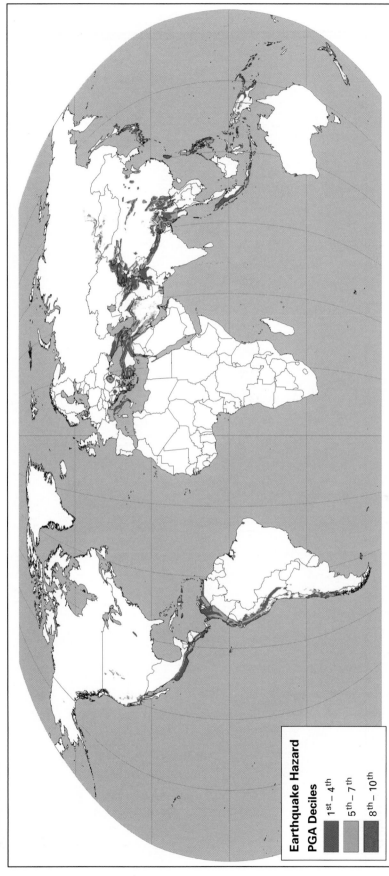

Figure 4.1. Distribution of Hazardous Areas by Hazard Type
d) Earthquakes (pga)

Earthquake Hazard
PGA Deciles

1st – 4th

5th – 7th

8th – 10th

Figure 4.1. Distribution of Hazardous Areas by Hazard Type
e) Earthquakes (con't)

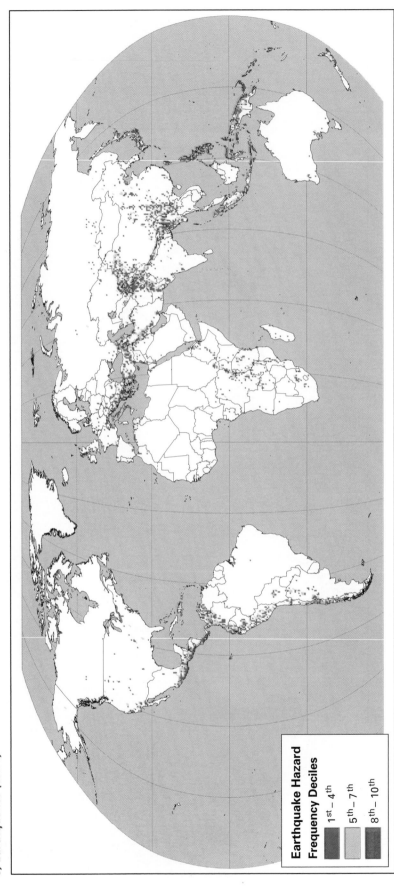

Earthquake Hazard Frequency Deciles

1st – 4th

5th – 7th

8th – 10th

Figure 4.1. Distribution of Hazardous Areas by Hazard Type
f) Volcanoes

Volcano Hazard Deciles

1st – 4th
5th – 7th
8th – 10th

Figure 4.1. Distribution of Hazardous Areas by Hazard Type
g) Landslides

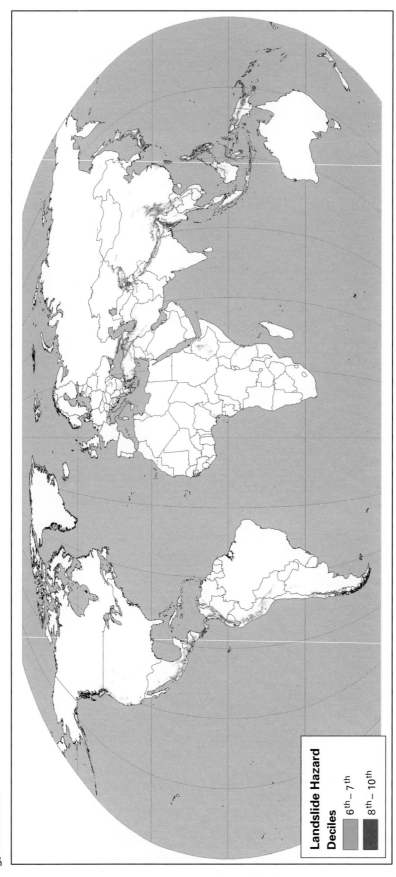

Landslide Hazard
Deciles

6th– 7th

8th– 10th

Table 4.1.   **Characteristics of High-Hazard Areas by Hazard: Top Three Deciles**

Hazard	*Land Area (10^6 km²)*	*Population (10^6)*	*GDP (10^9 \$)*	*Agricultural GDP (10^9 \$)*	*Road/Rail Length (10^3 km)*
Cyclones	2.5	553	7,053	81	275
Drought	12.9	1,094	5,319	252	1,078
Floods	11.5	2,283	14,670	371	1,191
Earthquakes	2.9	328	3,425	50	242
Volcanoes	0.1	45	240	3	14
Landslides	0.8	66	782	10	45
Percent of World					
Cyclones	1.9%	9.1%	16.0%	5.9%	3.5%
Drought	9.8%	18.1%	12.0%	18.5%	13.6%
Floods	8.8%	37.7%	33.2%	27.2%	15.0%
Earthquakes	2.2%	5.4%	7.8%	3.7%	3.1%
Volcanoes	0.1%	0.8%	0.5%	0.2%	0.2%
Landslides	0.6%	1.1%	1.8%	0.8%	0.6%

more than 2 billion people (38 percent). These flood-prone regions include large areas of the midwestern United States, Central America, coastal South America, Europe, eastern Africa, northeast India and Bangladesh, China, the Korean peninsula, Southeast Asia, Indonesia, and the Philippines. The high frequency of flooding in Bangladesh and surrounding areas presumably reflects the influence of tropical storms, and appears to compensate to some degree for the weak identification of storm-related hazard in the cyclone data noted previously. The very large areas of China and other parts of Asia highlighted in red may stem in part from the crude georeferencing of flood reports in these areas, which in turn may overemphasize these densely populated areas. On the other hand, it is certainly clear that large areas of China, such as the Yangtze River basin, are subject to significant flood risk affecting large areas and large populations.

These areas also represent relatively high concentrations of GDP and agricultural value added, more than triple the average for the world. This is consistent with the idea that flood-prone areas are also areas of more intensive agricultural production and development.

Earthquakes

We have examined two different data sets for assessing earthquake hazards, the first based on the GSHAP data set and the second on counts of reported earthquake activity. The latter is based on a relatively limited 27-year record, so the overall area affected is more limited than that captured by the GSHAP data set. The GSHAP data set reflects expert judgment on the potential severity of earthquakes at a fixed probability level (10 percent in 50 years), taking into account scientific understanding of earthquake processes (as of about 1999, the end of the GSHAP activity) as well as longer periods of record in many areas of the world.

Approximately 10 million square kilometers of land, about 7.5 percent of the total world land area, is estimated to have a 10 percent probability of pga of at least 2 m/s² in a 50-year period. An estimated 1.2 billion people, or about 20 percent of world population, live in these areas around the year 2000.

Cells in the top three deciles of pga values had a land area of nearly three million square kilometers and a total population of more than 300 million people, about 5 percent of total world population, and an associated GDP of nearly 8 percent. Areas of relatively high hazard include the western coast of the United States, Central America, and the western coast of South America, as well as much of southern Europe, Turkey, the Islamic Republic of Iran, central Asia, southwest China, Nepal, Taiwan (China), Japan, the Philippines, and New Zealand. Road and rail lengths in these areas are about average, roughly 240,000 kilometers or about 3 percent of the total world transportation length.

Volcanoes

Volcanoes are the most spatially concentrated hazard of the six considered here, affecting only 400,000 square kilometers and 93 million people in all nonzero cells, mainly in Japan, the Philippines, Indonesia, the United States, Mexico, Central America, Colombia, Ecuador, and Chile. For the top three deciles (red areas of Figure 4.1f), only 114,000 square kilometers and 45 million people are included. These areas are much more densely populated than average and have high GDP densities, about six times the world average, though this is partly because of Japan's inclusion. The agricultural value associated with these volcanic areas is about 2.7 times the world average density. No attempt has been made here to identify buffers around the volcanoes or to address possible impacts from a larger scale eruption (for example, ash deposits over a large area).

Landslides

The NGI index of landslides and snow avalanches ranges in value from 1 to 9 (Nadim and Kjekstad, in process; NGI 2004). However, values of 4 or less are considered very low in frequency. We have mapped the cells using deciles, but the overall map of NGI classes 5–9 corresponds closely with the decile groupings shown in Figure 4.1g. Note that this map differs from the map shown in Figure 7.1 of NGI (2004), primarily because of the masking of unpopulated, nonagricultural areas.

The total land area subject to landslides is about 3.7 million square kilometers with a population of nearly 300 million, or 5 percent of total world population. The relatively high-risk areas (top three deciles) cover about 820,000 square kilometers with an estimated population of 66 million. GDP density is higher than average, but agricultural value added and road and rail length are about average.

Single-Hazard Analysis of Exposure

The individual hazard maps demonstrate considerable diversity in the distribution of relatively high hazard areas. Cyclones, droughts, and floods cover large,

often overlapping areas, especially in parts of eastern North America, Central America, and Asia. Along with landslides, they represent relatively frequent events with a range of intensities.

The earthquake hazard is also dispersed, but the probability of a major earthquake is comparatively low over a longer period. On the other hand, when exposure and vulnerability are high, significant numbers of deaths and considerable damage in a concentrated area can result, as evidenced by the December 2003 earthquake in the Islamic Republic of Iran. The other geophysical hazard, volcanoes, is confined to much smaller and clearly defined regions. Large-scale volcanic events are relatively rare, but sometimes have substantial impacts on nearby populations through lava flows, ash deposition, pyroclastic events, and other phenomena.

As noted above, the highest hazard areas often have higher-than-average densities of population, GDP, agricultural GDP, and transportation length. As shown in Figures 4.2a–d, this is generally the case for areas affected by cyclones, volcanoes, and floods. The densities of these socioeconomic variables do not vary significantly with drought and earthquake deciles, though the slight increase in GDP density and decrease in agriculture GDP and transportation densities for the highest earthquake decile is of interest. GDP density increases but transportation density decreases at higher levels of landslide hazard.

In Appendix A.2, we weight each hazard distribution by population density to create spatial distributions of population hazard exposure. Since population density varies significantly across the grid cells included in the analysis—from the minimum value of five people per square kilometer to more than 30,000 people per square kilometer—simple weighting of the hazard values by population density would result in the highest exposure deciles being simply the high population density areas, including those exposed to only moderate levels of hazard.

The alternative approach presented in Appendix A.2 is therefore to divide grid cells into deciles based on population density alone and to use the resulting index (1–10) to weight each hazard distribution. A grid cell with a drought decile value of 8 might therefore have a drought population-exposure index ranging from 8 to 80. Because of the average increase in population density at higher hazard levels noted above, we expect that most high hazard cells will generally be classified as high on the hazard population-exposure index as well.

In brief, the patterns for population hazard exposure remain very similar to those for the unweighted hazard distributions. Population totals and densities increase to some degree in the most hazardous areas over the population totals and densities in hazardous areas as defined by the unweighted, hazard-only index.

Figure 4.2. Exposure Measures by Hazard Decile
a) Population Density

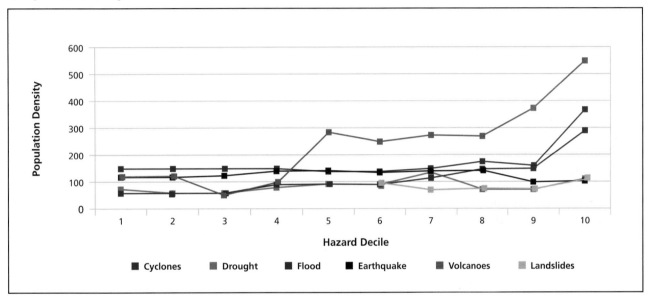

Figure 4.2. Exposure Measures by Hazard Decile
b) GDP Density

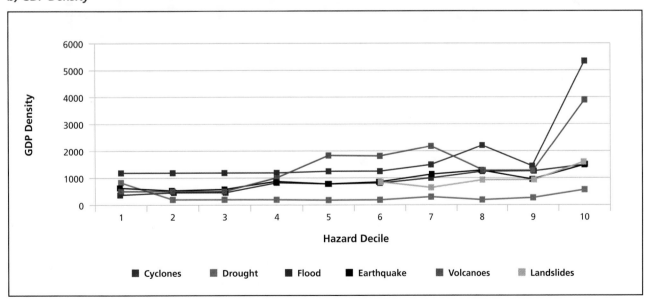

Figure 4.2. Exposure Measures by Hazard Decile
c) Agriculture GDP Density

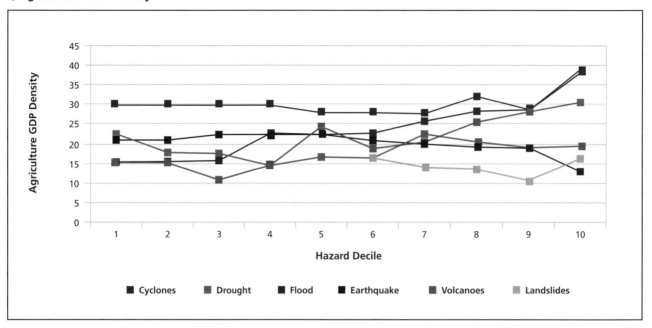

Figure 4.2. Exposure Measures by Hazard Decile
d) Transportation Length Density

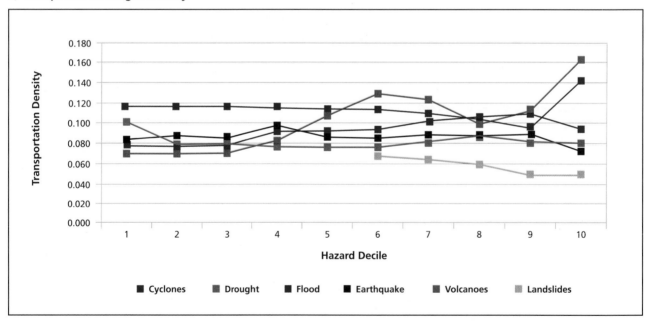

Chapter 5
Multihazard Exposure Analysis

Under ideal circumstances, it would be possible to determine precisely the spatial and temporal distributions of risk for specific locations and time periods by comparing, for different natural hazards, the estimated levels of particular hazards, and exposure and vulnerability to those hazards. Unfortunately, many factors make this difficult.

First, natural hazards differ greatly in their temporal and spatial patterns of occurrence. To estimate the risk of volcanic hazards, for example, one would need records over many centuries or even millennia to ascertain the frequency of events with any confidence. Over comparable time periods, higher frequency events such as droughts and floods might change significantly because of climate trends. During these periods, population exposure and vulnerability also change, which makes prediction of expected losses over time difficult.

Second, as noted previously, we often lack comparable, detailed data about the spatial location and extent of hazards, their intensity and duration, and other characteristics that can interact with exposure and vulnerability. Such data limitations make probability and risk estimates less certain and comparisons between hazards more difficult.

Finally, there are normative aspects to comparing risks. For example, some individuals or groups may value future potential losses differently than present potential losses, depending on their personal or social "discount rates" (Schneider and Chen 1980). Similarly, individuals or groups may have disparate views on mortality, morbidity, economic losses, and social impacts, and may disagree, for example, on the relative costs of loss of life as opposed to reduction in economic well-being. Some may also have different preferences regarding different types of risks, such as large-scale catastrophic risks, risks that come with significant perceived bene-fits (for example, living along coasts), or risks that lead to long-term irreversible impacts.

Despite these problems, it is still important to characterize risks of specific types of losses associated with natural hazards as objectively as possible, making clear alternative assumptions that may lead to different quantitative or qualitative results. Given the data limitations, it is important to proceed systematically from simpler to more complex methods for multihazard analysis. In this section, we develop simple multihazard indexes based solely on hazard probability and exposure data. In Chapter 6, we address the more difficult problem of incorporating vulnerability in order to compare risk levels from the perspective of both mortality and economic loss.

Simple Multihazard Index

In this section, we construct a simple multihazard index by summing category values between 8 and 10 across all six natural hazards. This results in a multihazard index that reflects the number of hazards considered relatively significant in a particular grid cell. Cells that are in the highest decile for multiple hazards will also rank slightly higher than those composed of slightly lower single-hazard decile values.

Total area, population, and other exposure characteristics by the combined hazards are summarized in Table 5.1. The overall global map is shown in Figure 5.1, and a version based on type of hazard is given in Figure 1.1. Detailed regional maps are provided in Figure 5.2.

Areas exposed to three to five hazards fall mostly along the west coasts of North, Central, and South America, mountain regions of Central and South Asia, and western Pacific coastlines. These are all areas charac-

Table 5.1. Summary Statistics for the Simple Multihazard Index

No. of Hazards	Index Values	Land Area (10⁶ km²)	Population (10⁶)	GDP (10⁹ $)	Agricultural GDP (10⁹ $)	Road/Rail Length (10³ km)
0	0	43.6	2,546.0	19,702	693	3,840
1	8–10	21.4	2,645.2	17,424	522	2,048
2	16–20	3.4	687.0	4,825	97	297
3–5	24–50	0.5	105.4	1,312	11	41
Percent of world						
0		33.4%	42.1%	44.6%	50.9%	48.5%
1		16.4%	43.7%	39.4%	38.4%	25.9%
2		2.6%	11.3%	10.9%	7.2%	3.8%
3–5		0.4%	1.7%	3.0%	0.8%	0.5%

terized by high relative susceptibility to both geophysical and hydro-meteorological hazards (yellow and red areas of Figure 1.1). These areas encompass, or are in close proximity to, major cities such as San Francisco, Guatemala, Managua, Quito, San Jose, Santiago, Manila, Taipei, and Tokyo. Although the total land area affected is relatively small, under 500,000 square kilometers, more than 100 million people live in these areas, associated with about 3 percent of total GDP.

Much larger areas and populations are exposed to two hazards. Nearly 800 million people, or 13 percent of the world's population, live in grid cells that have relatively high exposure to two or more different hazards. Areas affected by two hazards cover much of the California coast and portions of the Gulf Coast and Caribbean, areas of the Horn of Africa and Madagascar, and much of the Chinese coast and the Korean Peninsula (yellow areas in Figure 1.1).

Overall, more than half of the world's population lives in areas subject to at least one hazard at a significant level, on just under 20 percent of the world's land area. This finding is driven primarily by the wider extent of drought and flood in the database and therefore the larger number of cells classified in the top three deciles. As for most of the single hazards, population, GDP, and transportation length are concentrated in the more hazardous areas. However, the effect is less pronounced for the transportation measure.

These multihazard distributions may help hazard managers primarily concerned with one hazard to understand how much their area is also susceptible to other hazards. In Table 5.2, for example, the total area exposed to cyclones is assessed in terms of overlapping hazards. This table indicates that floods have the strongest overlap with cyclones: some one-third of the area affected by cyclones is also affected by floods. These areas include some 60 percent of the total population exposed to cyclones, which totals over 300 million people. About 9 percent of the cyclone-prone area overlaps with areas of relatively high drought, and another 9 percent overlaps with relatively high earthquake hazards. It is striking that the former areas are much less densely populated than the latter. This likely stems from the high exposure of urban areas in Japan, the Philippines, and Taiwan (China) to both cyclones and earthquakes, as compared with more rural overlapping cyclone and drought regions in Madagascar, Vietnam, and eastern Mexico. Landslides are also an issue for 5 percent of the land area and about 4 percent of the population. Volcanoes remain a localized problem. Note that the land area and population estimates for the five hazards include areas and population exposed to more than two hazards.

Similar "bi-hazard" profiles may be generated for each hazard, globally and regionally, providing a simple way to inform analysts and decision makers about the potential importance of multihazard analysis from their regional and sectoral perspectives.

Another application of these data is to identify areas that have comparable hazard profiles on multiple dimensions of hazard probability and exposure. For example, an analyst or decision maker might wish to identify comparable areas with a particular combination of exposures to cyclone and drought within a particular range of population or GDP density. Such an analyst might find it useful to compare hazard impacts and response for the three areas on the three different continents noted above that face both cyclone and drought.

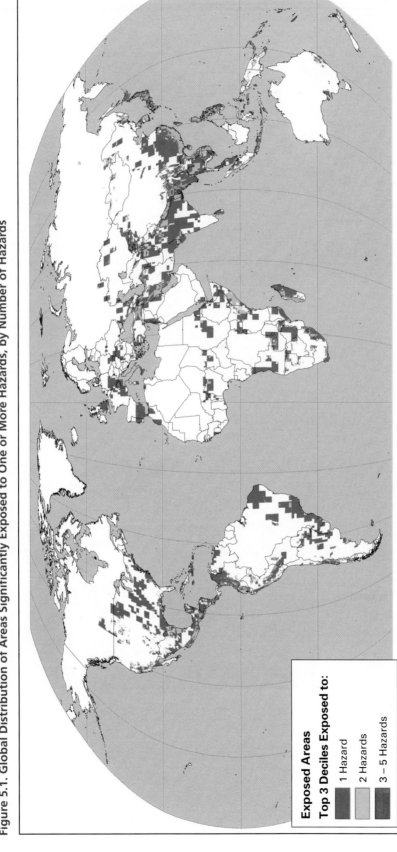

Figure 5.1. Global Distribution of Areas Significantly Exposed to One or More Hazards, by Number of Hazards

Figure 5.2. Detailed View of Multihazard Areas
a) Western Hemisphere

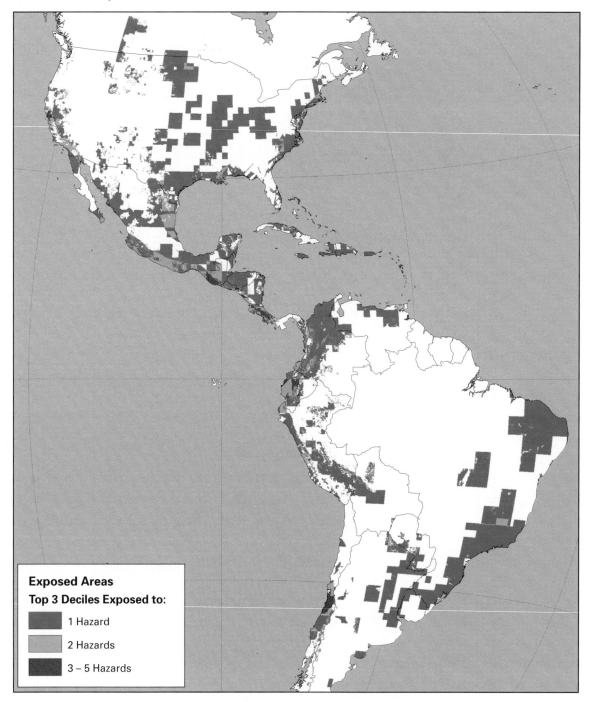

Figure 5.2. Detailed View of Multihazard Areas
b) Asia/Pacific

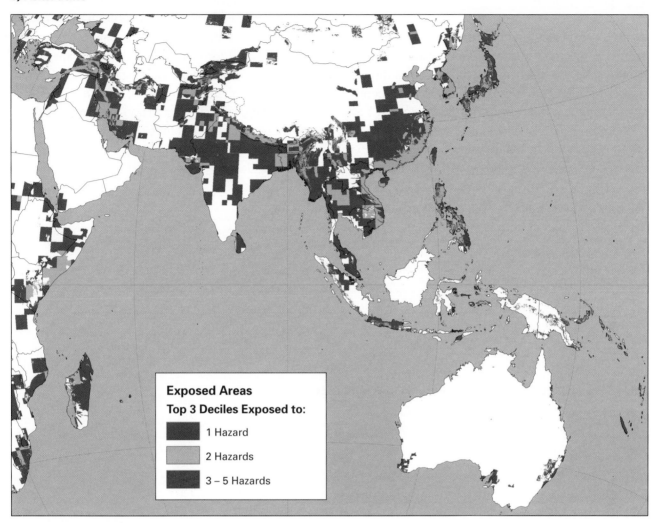

Reclassification of Multihazard Areas by Population Density

As in the case of the single-hazard assessment, it is important to modify the wide range of population density to avoid giving too much weight to the spatial distribution of population. In this case, we divide the population density into three categories: low (between 5 and 14.49 people per square kilometer); medium (14.5 to 51.49 people per square kilometer); and high (51.5 or more people per square kilometer)(Figure 5.3).

Table 5.3 indicates that high population density areas that coincide with the highest three deciles of two or more hazards include more than 650 million people living on 1.75 million square kilometers. This underscores the need for using a multihazard management approach in densely populated regions, where interactions among urban development, social displacement, and overlapping hazards could lead to areas of enhanced risk at finer scales of resolution.

Table 5.2. Hazard Profile for High-Cyclone Exposed Areas

	Cyclones	Drought	Floods	Earthquakes	Volcanoes	Landslides
Land Area (10^3 km²)	2,452	229	822	220	23	117
Population (10^6)	552.5	11.6	331.8	91.3	5.9	21.7
Population Density	225	51	403	416	260	185
Percent of Total Cyclone Area/Population						
Land Area	100%	9.3%	33.5%	9.0%	0.9%	4.8%
Population	100%	2.1%	60.1%	16.5%	1.1%	3.9%

Table 5.3. Summary Statistics for the Population-Weighted Multihazard Index

Population Density Class	No. of Hazards	Land Area (millions of km²)	Population (millions)	GDP (billions of $)	Agricultural GDP (billions of $)
High	0	8.8	2,078.8	15,351	338
	1	8.1	2,440.6	15,285	337
	2	1.8	653.1	4,394	77
	3–5	0.3	100.7	1,177	8
Medium	0	11.7	324.3	2,870	159
	1	5.3	152.4	1,464	79
	2	0.8	25.9	323	13
	3–5	0.1	4.1	103	2
Low	0	14.1	123.3	1,137	93
	1	5.1	46.0	540	54
	2	0.6	5.6	98	5
	3–5	0.1	0.6	31	1

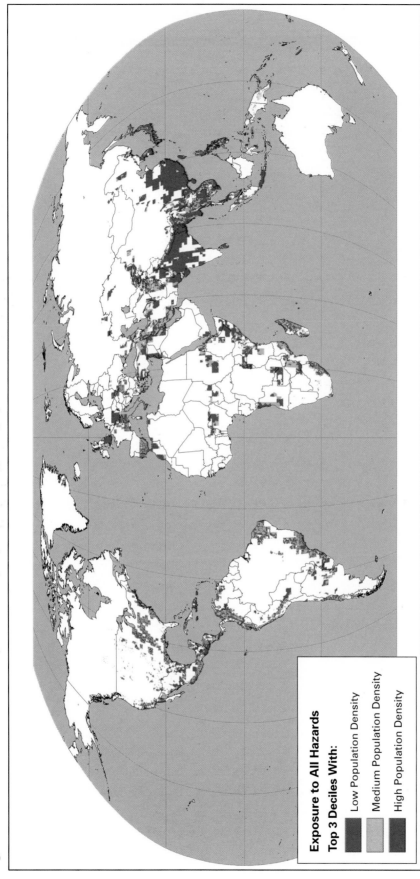

Figure 5.3. Global Distribution of Multiple Hazards by Population Density Category

Exposure to All Hazards
Top 3 Deciles With:
Low Population Density
Medium Population Density
High Population Density

Chapter 6
Multihazard Risk Assessment

Disaster risks are a function of hazard exposure and vulnerability. For a given level of hazard, risks of death and losses can differ greatly because of differences in exposure and vulnerability. For example, drought hazards of the same apparent magnitude and affecting the same numbers of people may be associated with high mortality and small absolute economic losses in developing countries, but with low mortality and large absolute economic losses in industrialized countries. In the absence of vulnerability information, risk indexes based solely on relative measures of hazard and exposure could fail to identify relatively modest risks posed by some natural hazards compared with much more severe risks posed by others.

In this section, therefore, we assess global risks of mortality and economic losses by incorporating estimated vulnerability by hazard, region, and country wealth status. Although data on vulnerability are aggregated and limited, incorporating such data into the analysis allows us to identify single- and multi-hazard-disaster risk hotspots, incorporating all sources of disaster causality.

Derivation of Vulnerability Coefficients

In the following analysis, we weight the value of population or GDP exposure to each hazard for each grid cell by a vulnerability coefficient to obtain an estimate of risk. The vulnerability weights are based on historical losses in previous disasters. There are two sets of weights: one derived from historical mortality and the other from historical economic losses. The mortality weights are applied to population exposure to obtain mortality risks; the economic loss weights are applied to GDP per unit area exposure to obtain economic loss risks. In each case, we calculate weights for each hazard, stratified by region and the wealth of the country in which the losses occurred. To assign the wealth status for each country, we used standard World Bank classifications based on GDP in 2000 (Appendix A.3).

We used historical losses as recorded in EM-DAT across all events from 1981 through 2000 for each hazard type to obtain mortality and economic loss weights for each hazard across each region for four wealth classes within regions (Tables 6.1 and 6.2). The weights are an aggregate index of relative losses within each region and country wealth class for each hazard over the 20-year period.

A high value in Table 6.1 or 6.2 indicates relatively high historical losses for a given combination of hazard and region/wealth class combination; a low value indicates relatively low rates of historical losses. Interestingly, the highest historical loss rates are not always in the lowest income countries. This suggests that the truism that the poor are always the most vulnerable may be an oversimplification. Although the data for drought in Africa in Table 6.1 (mortality) certainly reinforce this perception, in other instances the middle- or even upper-income countries have historically experienced the highest rates of losses. Some middle-income countries, for example, might have a relatively high value of economic assets at risk, without having instituted adequate measures to reduce the vulnerability of those assets during hazard events.

The vulnerability coefficients given in Tables 6.1 and 6.2 not only affect the relative significance of each hazard across the regions and country groupings, but also characterize the relative significance of the six hazards within each group. Thus, for example, mortality rates associated with cyclones are generally 3 to 20 times larger than those associated with floods in most low-income

Table 6.1. Mortality-Related Vulnerability Coefficients

Region and Wealth Status	Cyclones	Drought	Earthquakes	Floods	Landslides	Volcanoes
Africa						
Low	5.06	118.97		1.51	0.95	79.10
Lower middle	59.35	1.10		3.10	0.00	0.00
Upper middle	0.57	0.00		2.18		
High	5.10	0.00				0.00
East Asia and the Pacific						
Low	10.17	0.42	2.60	2.24	2.08	0.79
Lower middle	5.03	0.15	3.17	2.22	4.74	13.20
Upper middle	39.22	0.00		0.51	23.31	
High	1.33	0.00	5.48	1.10	1.20	0.51
Europe and Central Asia						
Low		0.00	0.75	2.82	5.69	
Lower middle	2.50	0.00	62.16	0.67	1.46	0.00
Upper middle		0.00	0.00	0.33	0.00	
High	1.65	0.00	1.77	0.25	2.67	0.00
Latin America and the Caribbean						
Low	39.72	0.00	4.22	2.36	0.00	0.12
Lower middle	44.16	0.00	3.24	4.44	8.53	231.68
Upper middle	4.27	0.01	13.86	11.21	4.24	1.62
High	3.26	0.00	0.00	0.00	0.00	0.00
Middle East and North Africa						
Low		0.00		5.81		0.00
Lower middle		0.00	271.25	5.11	2.54	
Upper middle		0.00	0.00	0.54	1.91	0.00
High	0.00	0.00	0.00	0.19		
North America						
High	1.01	0.00	0.39	0.19	0.00	0.00
South Asia						
Low	64.52	0.04	8.04	3.90	7.04	
Lower middle	0.20	0.00				
Upper middle						
High		0.00				

Note: These coefficients are based on hazard-specific historical mortality rates (persons killed during 1981 through 2000 per 100,000 persons in 2000) and are used to weight population exposure to estimate mortality risk. Blank cells indicate insignificant recorded historical losses. The number of historical events available to calculate each weight varies, with some weights based on as few as five to ten events.

Table 6.2. Economic Loss-Related Vulnerability Coefficients

Region and Wealth Status	Cyclones	Drought	Earthquakes	Floods	Landslides	Volcanoes
Africa						
Low	38.97	5.55		0.65	0.00	0.00
Lower middle	127.01	0.01		2.33	0.00	0.00
Upper middle	18.49	9.88		0.00		
High	5.24	0.00				0.00
East Asia and the Pacific						
Low	59.47	0.66	0.92	25.97	0.07	7.58
Lower middle	8.62	0.54	10.72	17.45	0.08	12.02
Upper middle	953.20	0.00		0.07	0.00	
High	4.02	8.54	47.97	1.53	0.17	0.00
Europe and Central Asia						
Low		4.52	16.34	5.56	3.80	
Lower middle	0.00	0.76	82.12	24.96	4.23	0.00
Upper middle		4.13	0.00	10.13	0.00	
High	24.04	3.29	19.23	4.23	4.65	0.31
Latin America and the Caribbean						
Low	71.65	7.50	2.23	0.36	0.00	0.17
Lower middle	48.84	2.74	8.82	7.04	3.97	22.94
Upper middle	14.48	1.28	11.72	5.88	1.04	0.37
High	104.27	0.00	0.00	0.00	0.00	0.00
Middle East and North Africa						
Low		0.00		168.87		0.00
Lower middle		9.35	38.98	5.90	0.00	
Upper middle	0.00	0.00	0.00	10.60	0.00	0.00
High		1.03	0.00	0.00		
North America						
High	13.00	0.97	30.82	2.84	0.00	0.00
South Asia						
Low	26.64	0.18	1.33	7.00	0.07	
Lower middle	0.00	0.00		5.26		
Upper middle						
High		0.00				

Note: These coefficients are based on hazard-specific historical economic rates (economic losses per $100,000 GDP in 2000 during 1981 through 2000) and are used to weight GDP exposure to obtain economic loss risks. Blank cells indicate insignificant recorded historical losses. The number of historical events available to calculate each weight varies, with some weights based on as few as five to ten events.

countries in Africa, Asia, and Latin America and in high-income areas of Europe and North America. Drought has minimal impact on mortality relative to other hazards, except in low-income Africa.

Aggregating across more than 6,000 entries in EM-DAT for this period helps compensate for missing data and reporting inaccuracies. The aggregate indexes are broadly reflective of patterns across hundreds of events rather than dependent on accurate loss estimations for individual events. This is particularly important in case of economic losses, since economic losses are unevenly recorded in EM-DAT. Only 30 percent of the entries in EM-DAT from 1981 through 2000 contain data on economic losses, and these economic loss data were assessed using nonstandardized methodologies.

The procedure for assessing mortality and economic loss risks for each grid cell was similar. In the case of mortality risks, the weights were based on historical mortality and applied to population exposure values at each grid point (Box 6.1). The derivation of economic loss risk is the same, with two exceptions: (1) the unit of analysis is GDP per unit area rather than population density, and (2) loss weights are based on historical economic losses rather than on historical mortality.

The resulting regional differences in loss risks are in part due to regional differences in population density, in the size of affected areas, and in the degree of hazard. But they also reflect differences in vulnerability. For instance, earthquakes in Japan tend to result in lower mortality rates than in many developing countries thanks to better enforcement of building codes, better emergency response, and the generally high level of preparedness.

In the above series of steps (see Box 6.1 for more detail), we assume that mortality within a given region is not uniformly distributed but rather is influenced by the frequency (and ideally, severity) of hazard events that have occurred in the region. We therefore allocate more of the region's total mortality to places with a higher apparent degree of hazard.

Rather than applying a constant mortality rate to a region's population, we generate an accumulated mortality by multiplying the mortality rate by the severity measure for each hazard. Since the degree of hazard for each of the six hazards is measured on a different scale (for example, frequency counts for droughts versus probability index values for landslides), the accumulated mortality numbers are not easily comparable across hazards. Before combining the hazards into a multihazard index that reflects total estimated impacts from all disaster types, we apply a uniform adjustment to all values within a given region such that the total hazard-specific mortality for all places in the region equals the actual number recorded in EM-DAT. The combined, mortality-weighted multihazard index is then simply the sum of the individual hazard mortality estimates for a given place.

Reporting actual mortality numbers would give an unrealistic impression of precision. Our more modest objective here is to provide a "relative" representation of disaster risk. For the purposes of cartographic output and interpretation, we therefore convert the resulting numbers into index values from 1 to 10 that correspond to deciles of the distribution of place-specific aggregate mortality.

The mortality-weighted multihazard index is strongly influenced by the choice of measure for the degree or severity of hazard. Ideally we would have sound rules for applying these measures and guiding the reallocation of mortality within regions. If we think of hazard mortality in epidemiological terms, we can think of measures of severity (frequency, duration, and magnitude, or combinations thereof) as the right-hand side term in a dose-response function that links the magnitude of an event to the resulting mortality. The form of this function could be linear or exponential (for example, stronger storms cause proportionally higher damage), or it could be defined by some kind of threshold value (for example, serious damage occurs only beyond a certain wind speed). Given a large enough set of records of hazard events and outcomes—combined with additional characteristics of the events and the exposed areas as controls—we could estimate a dose-response function empirically. This would provide a sounder empirical grounding of the proposed multihazard indicator and would also reduce the problem of including areas with relatively low disaster risk in the definition of exposed areas. Clearly this represents a promising direction for future work.

To extend the mortality-weighted approach to economic loss risk assessment, we use the geographically

Box 6.1. Risk Assessment Procedure for Both Mortality and Economic Losses, Illustrated by the Mortality Example.

1. We extract the appropriate measure of total global losses from 1981–2000 from EM-DAT (in the mortality case, the number of fatalities) by hazard h: M_h.

2. Using the GIS data on the extent of each hazard, we compute the total population estimated to live in the area affected by that hazard in the year 2000: P_h.

3. We then compute a simple mortality rate for the hazard: $r_h = M_h / P_h$. If we assume that the 1981–2000 period was representative, this rate is an estimate of the proportion of persons killed during a 20-year period in the area exposed to that hazard. Since the numbers are very small, they are expressed per 100,000 persons in 2000. Future revisions of the index could construct a mortality rate for the 20-year period based on annual rates which are computed using yearly mortality and population figures. As the results are intended only as an index of disaster risk, however, we believe that the computational simplification of using only end-of-period population is justified.

4. For each GIS grid cell i that falls into a hazard zone h, we compute the location-specific expected mortality by multiplying the global hazard-specific mortality rate by the population in that grid cell: $M_{hi} = r_h * P_h$. We do this for all six hazards, then compute a mortality-weighted multihazard index value for each grid cell:

$$Y_i = \sum_{h=1}^{6} P_{hi}.$$

This first estimate represents an unweighted index value that assumes that mortality rates are globally uniform and that hazard severity has no influence on the relative distribution of mortality. In the following steps we relax these assumptions.

5. If we denote the various combinations of region and country wealth class (see Table 6.2) by j, then the estimated mortality in a given grid cell is now $M_{hij} = r_{hj} * P_i$.

6. The global hazard data compiled for the analysis measures the degree of hazard in terms of frequency in most, although not all, cases (see Table 3.3). The various degree-of-hazard measures are used to redistribute the total regional mortality from EM-DAT across the grid cells in the area of the region exposed to each hazard. For example, if a grid cell were hit four times by a severe earthquake during the 20-year period, the regional mortality rate is multiplied by four to yield an accumulated mortality for that grid cell. More generally, if the degree of hazard measure is denoted by W, and assuming that the weighting scheme is identical across region/wealth-class combinations j, the accumulated mortality in the grid cell is: $M_{hij} = r_{hj} * W_{hi} * P_i$.

   Since the degree of hazard is not always measured on the same scale across hazards, simply adding up the resulting values would result in an index that could be unduly dominated by a hazard that happens to be measured on a scale with larger values. We therefore deflate the weighted hazard-specific mortality figures uniformly, so that the total mortality in each region adds up to the total recorded in EM-DAT. The resulting weighted mortality from hazard h in grid cell i and region/wealth-class combination j is thus:

$$M^*_{hij} = M_{hij} M_{hj} / \sum_{i=1}^{n} M_{hij},$$

where n is the number of grid cells in the area exposed to hazard h. Future revisions could be based on alternative definitions of severity such as wind speed and duration for storms or earthquake and volcanic eruption magnitudes.

7. A mortality-weighted multihazard disaster risk hotspot index can be calculated as the sum of the adjusted single-hazard mortalities in the grid cell across the six hazard types:

$$Y^*_i = \sum_{h=1}^{6} M^*_{hij}.$$

continued

Box 6.1. Risk Assessment Procedure for Both Mortality and Economic Losses, Illustrated by the Mortality Example *(continued)*

8. To avoid literal interpretation of the multihazard disaster risk hotspot index as the number of persons expected to be killed in a 20-year period and in recognition of the many limitations of the underlying data, we convert the resulting measure into an index from 1 to 10, classifying the global distribution of unmasked grid cell values into deciles.

referenced database of subnational GDP per unit area. Although the global GDP surface is less detailed than the population data set, it represents the best available disaggregated information on economic output. Carrying out the same steps as described above for mortality yields measures of economic losses per unit of GDP. Reallocation of economic losses within regions and country wealth classes is again guided by hazard-specific loss weights based on historical economic losses from EM-DAT. The resulting economic hotspots indicator for damage-weighted multihazard disaster risk reflects that although mortality impacts are lower in richer countries, economic losses for a given event are higher. For instance, a hurricane in southern Florida causes considerably more economic damage than a similar hurricane in poorer countries, since the value of real estate, infrastructure, and other economically productive assets is much higher in the United States. Of course, such damage is usually a higher proportion of regional and national income in developing countries than in industrial countries and is also higher relative to available resources for relief and reconstruction.

Single-Hazard Risk Assessment Results

Global results below are for risks of mortality- and economic loss-related outcomes by hazard type. Economic losses are presented both in aggregate terms and normalized relative to GDP density. Note that this normalization essentially removes the effect of GDP density, leaving the economic loss-related vulnerability coefficients applied to the underlying hazard distribution.

Cyclones

Not surprisingly, mortality risk for cyclones is highest along the Pacific and Indian coastlines and in the Caribbean and Central America (red areas of Figure 6.1a). Despite the low relative hazard shown for the Bay of Bengal in Figure 4.1a, when weighted by mortality, this area is ranked much higher in terms of risk. The picture changes somewhat in examining aggregate economic risk: the eastern United States and the United Kingdom show relatively high risk, and poor areas of Africa no longer rank in the top three deciles (Figure 6.1b). However, large portions of India and Asia remain relatively high in terms of aggregate economic risk. When normalized for GDP, Madagascar and neighboring areas reappear in the top three deciles, but China, Japan, and the Republic of Korea drop out (Figure 6.1c). The areas of significant risk in North and Central America and the Caribbean appear to shift slightly south.

Overall, one billion people, or about 18 percent of the world's population, live in areas at high risk of cyclone mortality (Table 6.3a). More than one-fourth of the world's GDP is at high risk of economic losses from cyclones (Table 6.3b).

Drought

The drought vulnerability coefficients for mortality shown in Table 6.1 give high weight to low-income African countries and very limited weight to other regions. This is reflected clearly in Figure 6.2a, in which all of the grid cells in the highest three deciles fall in Sub-Saharan Africa. In contrast, economic loss risks related to drought are much more dispersed (Figure 6.2b), with

Figure 6.1. Global Distribution of Cyclone Risk
a) Mortality

Cyclone Mortality
Risk Deciles

1st – 4th
5th – 7th
8th – 10th

Figure 6.1. Global Distribution of Cyclone Risk
b) Total Economic Loss

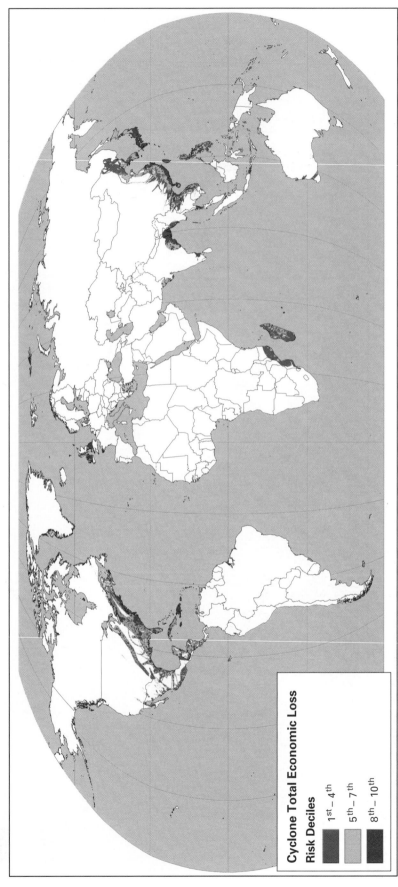

Cyclone Total Economic Loss

Risk Deciles

1st – 4th

5th – 7th

8th – 10th

Figure 6.1. Global Distribution of Cyclone Risk
c) Economic Loss as a Proportion of GDP Density

Cyclone Proportional
Economic Loss
Risk Deciles

1st – 4th
5th – 7th
8th – 10th

relatively significant risks on all continents. As indicated in Table 6.3b, these areas are heavily populated and important in terms of both economic and agricultural activity. Areas of Europe, Central America, and western Africa that seem to have only modest drought exposure (Figure 4.1b) appear to have higher overall risk. The distribution of drought-related losses normalized by GDP density (Figure 6.2c) reflects a middle ground between these extremes, with high relative losses in Sub-Saharan Africa, but also noticeable areas of high risk in Central and South America, southern Europe, the Middle East, the Republic of Korea, and southern Australia. Surprisingly, drought risk normalized by GDP density does not seem to be significant in South and Southeast Asia and China, despite their high reliance on agriculture. This could reflect underreporting of historical losses or low vulnerability to drought thanks to irrigation.

Floods

Application of the flood mortality vulnerability coefficients from Table 6.1 to global population flood exposure yields roughly the same spatial pattern as that of cyclone hazard frequency shown in Figure 4.1c. Minor differences include lower relative risk in the eastern United States, high relative risk in North Africa, and somewhat greater areas of high relative risk in India, China, and other parts of Asia (Figure 6.3a). Much of

Table 6.3. Characteristics of High-Risk Areas by Hazard

a) Top three deciles based on mortality

Hazard	Land Area (10^6 km^2)	Population (10^6)	GDP (10^9 $)	Agricultural GDP (10^9 $)	Road/Rail Length (10^3 km)
Cyclones	2.7	1,096	8,909	119	332
Drought	9.7	573	1,086	49	619
Floods	14.4	3,936	22,859	528	1,507
Earthquakes	2.9	865	5,282	89	334
Volcanoes	0.1	56	166	3	12
Landslides	1.1	215	1,431	23	87
Percent of World					
Cyclones	2.1%	18.1%	20.2%	8.8%	4.2%
Drought	7.5%	9.5%	2.5%	3.6%	7.8%
Floods	11.0%	65.0%	51.7%	38.8%	19.0%
Earthquakes	2.2%	14.3%	12.0%	6.5%	4.2%
Volcanoes	0.1%	0.9%	0.4%	0.2%	0.2%
Landslides	0.8%	3.6%	3.2%	1.7%	1.1%

b) Top three deciles based on economic losses

Hazard	Land Area (10^6 km^2)	Population (10^6)	GDP (10^9 $)	Agricultural GDP (10^9 $)	Road/Rail Length (10^3 km)
Cyclones	2.4	940	11,723	94	401
Drought	14.8	2,790	17,556	446	1,697
Floods	13.2	3,776	31,216	598	1,751
Earthquakes	2.8	614	7,032	86	381
Volcanoes	0.1	59	201	2	11
Landslides	0.9	124	2,077	20	110
Percent of World					
Cyclones	1.8%	15.5%	26.5%	6.9%	5.1%
Drought	11.3%	46.1%	39.7%	32.8%	21.4%
Floods	10.1%	62.4%	70.6%	43.9%	22.1%
Earthquakes	2.1%	10.1%	15.9%	6.3%	4.8%
Volcanoes	0.1%	1.0%	0.5%	0.2%	0.1%
Landslides	0.7%	2.1%	4.7%	1.5%	1.4%

Figure 6.2. Global Distribution of Drought Risk
a) Mortality

Drought Mortality
Risk Deciles

1st – 4th
5th – 7th
8th – 10th

Figure 6.2. Global Distribution of Drought Risk
b) Total Economic Loss

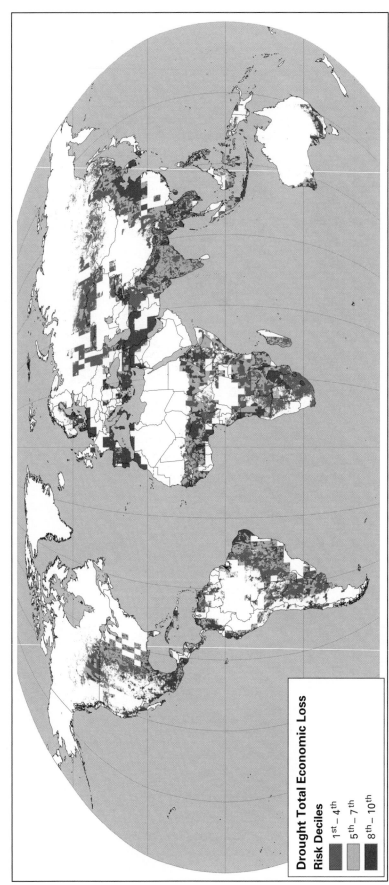

Drought Total Economic Loss
Risk Deciles

1st – 4th

5th – 7th

8th – 10th

Figure 6.2. Global Distribution of Drought Risk
c) Economic Loss as a Proportion of GDP Density

**Drought Proportional
Economic Loss
Risk Deciles**

1st – 4th

5th – 7th

8th – 10th

Asia and parts of Central and South America appear high in risk in terms of both mortality and economic loss (Figures 6.3a, b). This is true even after normalizing for GDP density (Figure 6.3c). Flood losses in the eastern United States appear relatively high in absolute terms but are relatively small when normalized against GDP. Economic risks in Africa are small in both absolute and relative terms. Collectively, very high proportions of the world appear to live in areas of high relative flood risk, and these areas have high total and agricultural GDP density (Table 6.3).

Earthquakes

The risks associated with earthquakes are high with respect to mortality and economic losses in most but not all areas where the hazard exists (Figure 4.1d). These areas include Central America, Venezuela, southern Europe, the Caucasus and Zagros mountain regions, Japan, and the Philippines (Figure 6.4a–c). The western United States is a region where economic risks are relatively high but mortality risks are low. Conversely, the Himalayan region stands out as an area of high mortality risk but minimal absolute and relative economic risk. Despite high earthquake hazard in Peru, Chile, and New Zealand, these areas do not appear especially at risk in terms of mortality and economic loss. In general, areas of high earthquake risk also have higher-than-

average population and GDP densities, comparable to those observed for cyclones and floods (Table 6.3).

Volcanoes

Less than one-third of the categories in Tables 6.1 and 6.2 have nonzero values for volcanoes, owing in part to the limited period of record for this relatively infrequent event. The result is that the areas of high relative risk from volcanoes are even more restricted than the volcano hazard shown in Figure 4.1f. In particular, the mortality and economic risks of volcanoes in Japan are not ranked in the top three deciles (Figure 6.5a–c). Risks are high in localized areas around volcanoes, with recent activity mainly in Central and South America, East Africa, and Indonesia. Only about 1 percent of the world's population lives in the top three deciles for volcanoes (Table 6.3).

Landslides

Landslide risks are significant in terms of both mortality and economic loss in Central America, northwestern South America, the Caucasus region, and Taiwan (China) (Figure 6.6a,b). Mortality-weighted risks are high in the Himalayan region, the Philippines, and Indonesia, but low in southern Europe and Japan (Figure 6.6a), where economic risks appear high (Figure 6.6b).

Figure 6.3. Global Distribution of Flood Risk
a) Mortality

**Flood Mortality
Risk Deciles**

1st – 4th
5th – 7th
8th – 10th

Figure 6.3. Global Distribution of Flood Risk
b) Total Economic Loss

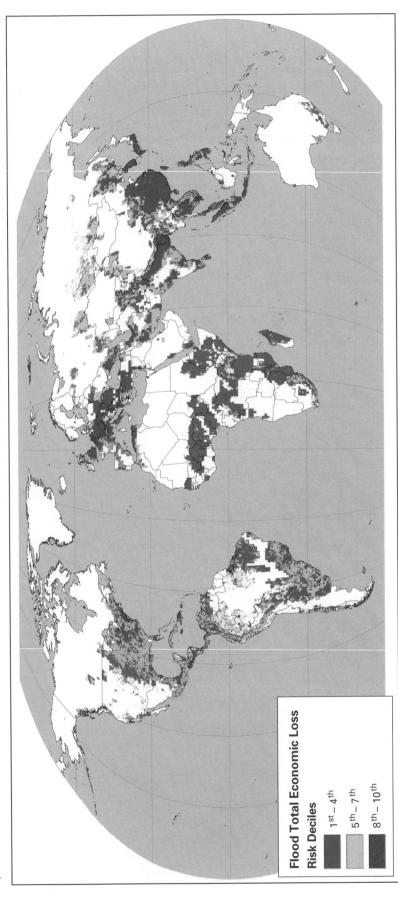

Flood Total Economic Loss
Risk Deciles

1st – 4th
5th – 7th
8th – 10th

Figure 6.3. Global Distribution of Flood Risk
c) Economic Loss as a Proportion of GDP Density

Flood Proportional Economic Loss Risk Deciles

1st – 4th
5th – 7th
8th – 10th

Figure 6.4. Global Distribution of Earthquake Risk
a) Mortality

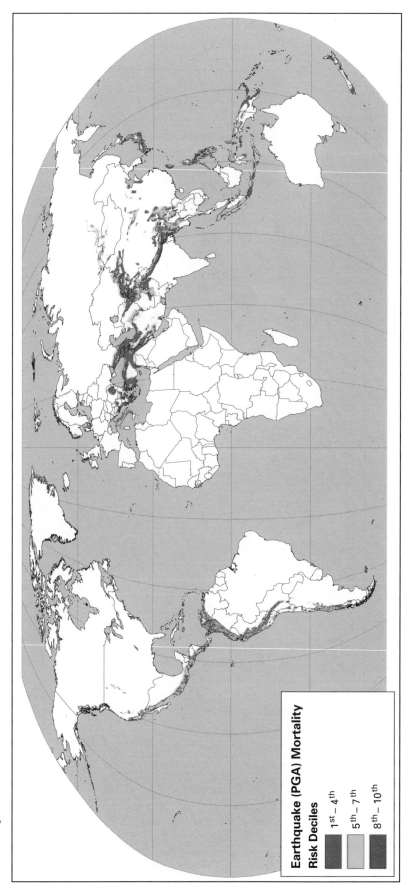

Earthquake (PGA) Mortality Risk Deciles

1st – 4th
5th – 7th
8th – 10th

Figure 6.4. Global Distribution of Earthquake Risk
b) Total Economic Loss

Earthquake (PGA) Total
Economic Loss
Risk Deciles

1st – 4th

5th – 7th

8th – 10th

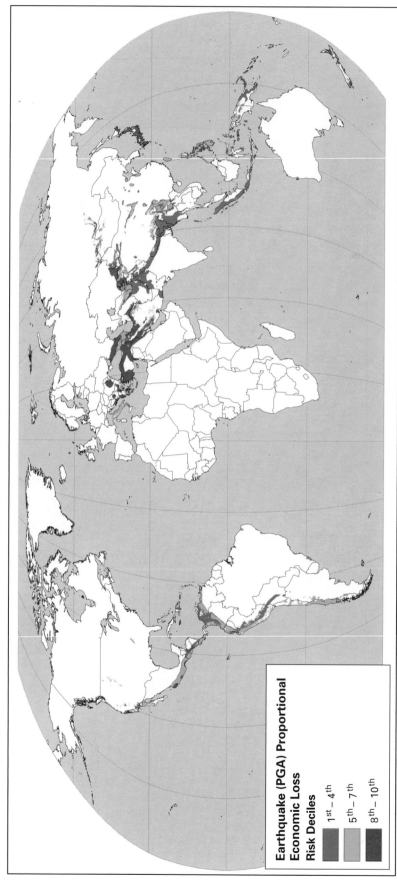

Figure 6.4. Global Distribution of Earthquake Risk
c) Economic Loss as a Proportion of GDP Density

Earthquake (PGA) Proportional Economic Loss Risk Deciles

$1^{st} - 4^{th}$
$5^{th} - 7^{th}$
$8^{th} - 10^{th}$

Figure 6.5. Global Distribution of Volcano Risk
a) Mortality

Volcano Mortality Risk Deciles

1st – 4th
5th – 7th
8th – 10th

Figure 6.5. Global Distribution of Volcano Risk
b) Total Economic Loss

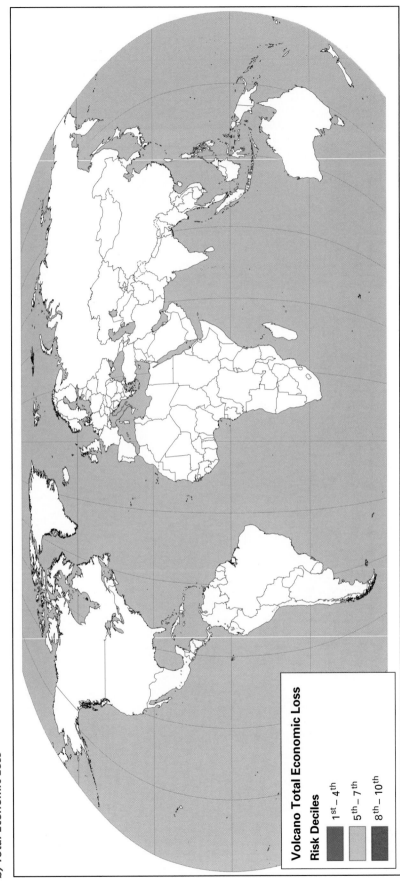

Volcano Total Economic Loss

Risk Deciles

1st – 4th

5th – 7th

8th – 10th

Figure 6.5. Global Distribution of Volcano Risk
c) Economic Loss as a Proportion of GDP Density

Volcano Proportional
Economic Loss
Risk Deciles

1st – 4th
5th – 7th
8th – 10th

Figure 6.6. Global Distribution of Landslide Risk
a) Mortality

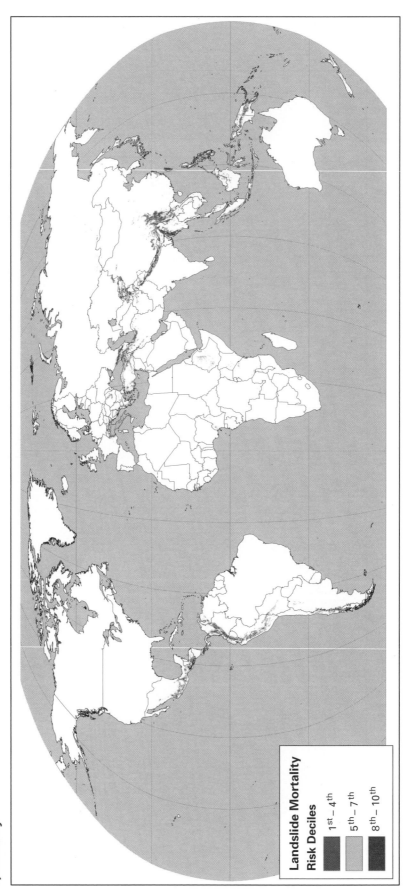

**Landslide Mortality
Risk Deciles**

1st – 4th

5th – 7th

8th – 10th

Figure 6.6. Global Distribution of Landslide Risk
b) Total Economic Loss

Figure 6.6. Global Distribution of Landslide Risk
c) Economic Loss as a Proportion of GDP Density

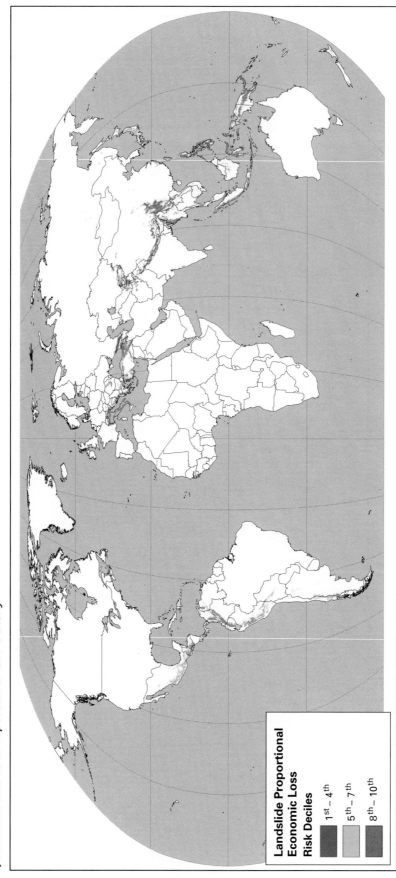

Landslide Proportional Economic Loss Risk Deciles

1st – 4th

5th – 7th

8th – 10th

Chapter 7
Multihazard Risk Assessment Results

Multihazard risks were calculated by summing the vulnerability-weighted single-hazard mortality and economic loss risk values for each grid cell across the six hazard types (Figure 7.1a–c). The strong drought-mortality signal in Sub-Saharan Africa shown in Figure 6.2a is strongly reflected in the multihazard map weighted by mortality (Figure 7.1a). So are the high-risk areas of Central America, the Caribbean, the Bay of Bengal, China, and the Philippines because of cyclones and floods. Areas of high earthquake and landslide risk are evident in Central America and Venezuela, Central Asia, the Himalayas, Japan, the Philippines, and Indonesia. Because of the relatively short period on which these rates are based, the vulnerability coefficients appear to give greater weight to the higher frequency hazards such as cyclones, drought, landslides, and floods. Mortality and economic losses are high in specific regions for earthquakes and volcanoes where they have occurred in 1981 through 2000, but may underestimate potential risks in other regions that face some degree of hazard.

Based on the mortality-weighted index, nearly one-fourth of total land area and more than three-fourths of the world's population are subject to a relatively high risk of mortality from one or more hazards. This reflects the higher population densities of areas that have experienced relatively high mortality during the past two decades according to EM-DAT. Only one-twentieth of the total land area (but about one-third of the population) is subject to higher mortality risk from two or more hazards. About 7 percent of the total population lives in areas at high mortality risk from three or more hazards (Table 7.1a). More than four-fifths of GDP is located in areas of relatively high economic risk subject to one or more hazards and more than half in high-risk areas subject to two or more hazards (Table 7.1b).

Another way to look at multihazard mortality risk is to show for how many hazards each mortality-risk grid cell value falls into the top three deciles (Figure 7.2a). This presentation makes it easier to discriminate within large regions where risks are evaluated as high across all hazards versus areas that are high risk for each hazard individually. Figures 1.2a–c show which types of hazards are prevalent at each location. As noted above, drought and combinations of drought and hydro-meteorological hazards dominate both mortality and economic losses in Sub-Saharan Africa. Geophysical hazards drive high mortality risk in western Asia, and combine with hydro-meteorological hazards in mountainous areas of Central America and Asia (Figure 1.2c). Drought is also an important driver of economic losses in many other countries, including Mexico, Spain, the Republic of Korea, and Australia.

The concentration of population and economic activity in areas at high relative risk from one or more hazards is of great interest from the viewpoint of national-level vulnerability and response capacity. As indicated in Table 1.2a, 35 countries have more than 5 percent of their population living in areas identified as relatively high in mortality risk from three or more hazards. Ninety-six countries have more than 10 percent of their population in areas at risk from two or more hazards (Table 1.2b and Figure 1.3). And 160 countries have more than one-fourth of their population in areas at relatively high mortality risk from one or more hazards (Figure 1.6). Similarly, many of the areas at higher risk of economic loss from multiple hazards are associated with higher-than-average densities of GDP, leading to a relatively high degree of exposure of economically productive areas (Table 7.2 and Figures 1.5 and 1.6).

81

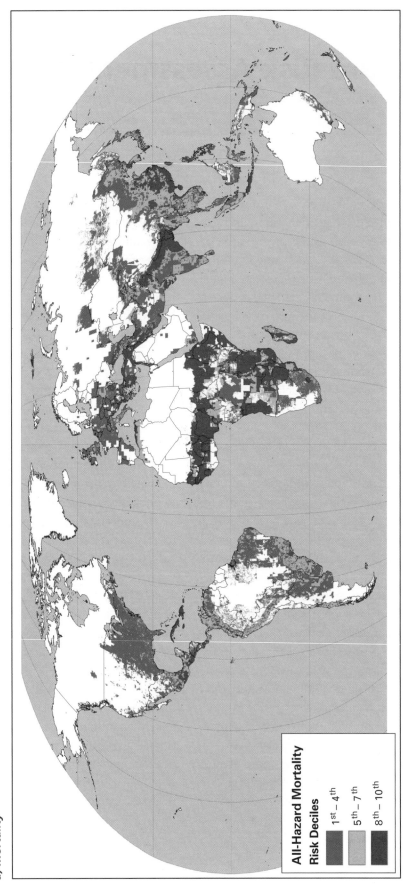

Figure 7.1. Global Distribution of Disaster Risk Hotspots for All Hazards
a) Mortality

**All-Hazard Mortality
Risk Deciles**

1st – 4th
5th – 7th
8th – 10th

Figure 7.1 Global Distribution of Disaster Risk Hotspots for All Hazards
b) Total Economic Loss

**All-Hazard Total Economic Loss
Risk Deciles**

1st – 4th
5th – 7th
8th – 10th

Figure 7.1 Global Distribution of Disaster Risk Hotspots for All Hazards
c) Economic Loss as a Proportion of GDP Density

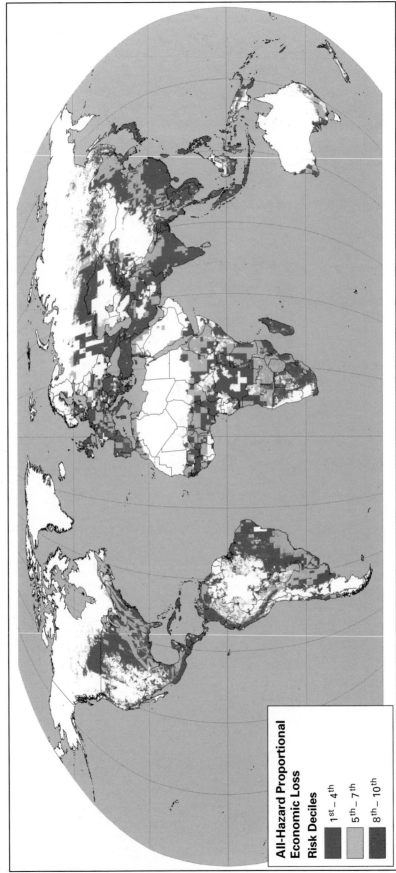

All-Hazard Proportional Economic Loss

Risk Deciles

1st – 4th

5th – 7th

8th – 10th

Figure 7.2 Global Distribution of Disaster Risk Hotspots by Number of Hazards
a) *Mortality*

Mortality Risk
Top 3 Deciles for:

1 Hazard

2 Hazards

3+ Hazards

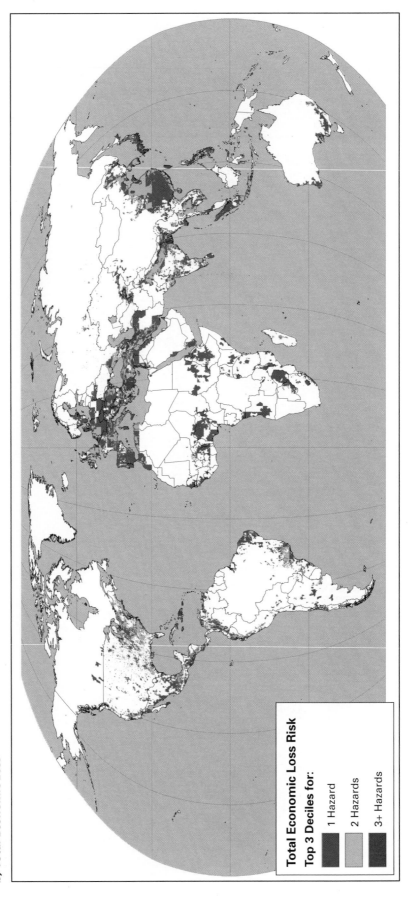

Figure 7.2 Global Distribution of Disaster Risk Hotspots by Number of Hazards
b) Total Economic Loss

Total Economic Loss Risk
Top 3 Deciles for:

1 Hazard

2 Hazards

3+ Hazards

Figure 7.2 Global Distribution of Disaster Risk Hotspots by Number of Hazards
c) Economic Loss as a Proportion of GDP Density

Proportional Economic Loss Risk
Top 3 Deciles for:

1 Hazard

2 Hazards

3+ Hazards

Table 7.1. Characteristics of High-Risk Disaster Hotspots

a) Top three deciles based on mortality

No. of Hazards	Land Area (10^6 km^2)	Population (10^6)	GDP (10^9 $)	Agricultural GDP (10^9 $)	Road/Rail Length (10^3 km)
1	22.8	2,602	15,648	470	1,890
2	6.3	1,629	9,276	184	614
3–5	0.9	432	3,219	28	109
Total	30.1	4,664	28,143	683	2,613
Percent of World					
1	17.4%	43.0%	35.4%	34.6%	23.9%
2	4.8%	26.9%	21.0%	13.5%	7.8%
3–5	0.7%	7.1%	7.3%	2.1%	1.4%
Total	23.0%	77.0%	63.7%	50.1%	33.0%

b) Top three deciles based on economic losses

No. of Hazards	Land Area (10^6 km^2)	Population (10^6)	GDP (10^9 $)	Agricultural GDP (10^9 $)	Road/Rail Length (10^3 km)
1	16.1	2,037	13,784	465	1,813
2	5.7	1,841	14,732	271	803
3-5	2.1	808	8,208	76	289
Total	23.9	4,686	36,724	812	2,905
Percent of World					
1	12.3%	33.7%	31.2%	34.1%	22.9%
2	4.3%	30.4%	33.3%	19.9%	10.1%
3-5	1.6%	13.3%	18.6%	5.6%	3.7%
Total	18.3%	77.4%	83.1%	59.6%	36.7%

Table 7.2. Countries at Relatively High Economic Risk from Multiple Hazards

a) Three or more hazards (top 33 based on GDP)

Country	Percent of Total Area at at Risk	Percent of Population in Areas at Risk	Percent of GDP in Areas at Risk
Taiwan, China	97.0	96.6	96.5
Dominican Rep.	77.0	90.7	92.0
Jamaica	79.6	87.7	87.8
El Salvador	64.5	84.1	85.4
Guatemala	39.5	83.4	83.3
Antigua and Barbuda	53.4	80.4	80.4
Japan	51.3	75.8	80.2
Costa Rica	38.6	77.9	80.1
Philippines	35.8	72.5	78.7
Colombia	10.0	69.0	73.0
Bangladesh	41.9	55.6	62.7
Chile	2.9	58.4	62.6
Korea, Rep. of	24.7	61.6	61.6
Turkey	37.7	50.4	55.6
Barbados	53.4	53.4	53.4
Guam	53.2	59.7	51.6
Uzbekistan	5.0	51.4	51.4
Ecuador	10.0	50.5	50.0
Venezuela	3.1	40.6	47.6
Peru	1.4	30.4	43.9
St. Kitts and Nevis	33.8	41.6	41.6
Iran, Islamic Republic of	15.4	45.2	39.8
Indonesia	3.0	30.5	34.2
Honduras	7.9	30.9	33.2
Greece	19.9	18.6	32.0
Albania	35.9	27.6	29.6
Mexico	6.9	31.1	29.2
Hong Kong, China	51.4	29.5	28.2
Tajikistan	1.2	27.1	27.1
Mozambique	0.0	1.3	23.7
Syrian Arab Rep.	7.5	24.3	21.2
Bolivia	0.4	20.3	20.8
United States	1.6	20.6	20.8

Table 7.2. Countries at Relatively High Economic Risk from Multiple Hazards

b) Two or more hazards (top 75 based on GDP)

Country	Percent of Total Area at Risk	Percent of Population in Areas at Risk	Percent of GDP in Areas at Risk
Taiwan, China	97.5	97.0	96.9
El Salvador	88.7	95.4	96.4
Jamaica	94.9	96.3	96.3
Dominican Rep.	87.2	94.7	95.6
Guatemala	52.7	92.1	92.2
Korea, Rep. of	82.8	92.2	91.5
Vietnam	33.2	75.7	89.4
Japan	65.6	86.5	89.0
Albania	86.4	88.6	88.5
Costa Rica	51.9	84.8	86.6
Colombia	21.2	84.7	86.6
Bangladesh	71.4	83.6	86.5
Philippines	50.3	81.3	85.2
Turkey	73.0	80.9	83.3
Trinidad and Tobago	66.7	82.4	83.1
Guam	83.6	84.5	82.6
Thailand	47.8	70.1	81.2
Antigua and Barbuda	53.4	80.4	80.4
Barbados	79.9	79.9	79.9
San Marino	66.7	55.3	73.1
Greece	65.5	73.7	72.6
Ecuador	24.4	73.6	72.2
Mexico	15.9	68.2	71.1
United States	9.3	67.5	68.7
Dominica	68.3	67.0	68.3
Nicaragua	21.6	68.7	67.9
Chile	5.2	64.9	67.7
Iran, Islamic Republic of	31.7	69.8	66.5
United Kingdom	38.6	64.5	66.0
Venezuela	4.9	61.2	65.9
Uzbekistan	9.3	65.6	65.5
St. Kitts and Nevis	0.0	52.8	64.9
Jordan	13.7	64.9	64.7
Argentina	1.8	57.4	63.2
South Africa	8.6	56.3	62.4
Tunisia	30.4	64.1	62.4
Indonesia	11.5	67.4	62.3
Cuba	22.5	56.7	57.9
China	13.1	49.8	56.6
Honduras	19.0	56.0	56.5
Haiti	44.4	47.9	56.0
Uruguay	3.0	55.0	55.0
Hong Kong, China	73.0	58.9	54.2
Netherlands	63.2	55.0	53.9
Peru	4.0	41.5	53.7
Liechtenstein	53.9	45.9	53.6
Kyrgyz Rep.	8.3	51.3	53.4
Montserrat	50.3	50.3	50.3
Romania	37.4	45.8	50.3
India	22.1	47.7	49.6
Algeria	3.1	49.3	48.3
Niue	48.1	48.1	48.1

continued

Table 7.2. Countries at Relatively High Economic Risk from Multiple Hazards, continued
b) Two or more hazards (top 75 based on GDP)

Country	Percent of Total Area at Risk	Percent of Population in Areas at Risk	Percent of GDP in Areas at Risk
Cyprus	50.4	60.5	47.4
Korea, Dem. People's Rep. of	27.6	44.5	46.3
Andorra	43.5	19.4	45.0
Australia	0.3	44.0	44.7
Paraguay	2.0	45.6	42.9
Azerbaijan	15.6	42.3	42.4
Pakistan	9.0	40.1	41.6
St. Vincent and the Grenadines	41.6	41.6	41.6
Georgia	4.4	40.5	41.0
Germany	26.8	38.9	40.3
Ireland	9.6	32.7	39.8
Italy	42.2	35.4	38.8
Macedonia, FYR	38.8	29.6	38.7
Tajikistan	4.1	38.2	38.3
Bolivia	1.0	36.6	37.7
Mozambique	0.0	1.9	37.3
Syrian Arab Rep.	14.9	34.4	36.8
Djibouti	1.9	31.7	35.3
Cambodia	9.1	31.3	34.5
New Zealand	1.6	33.9	33.7
Morocco	3.4	30.4	33.4
Canada	0.2	36.0	32.1
Bulgaria	29.3	31.6	30.0

Chapter 8
Case Studies

The Hotspots project is an effort to deepen understanding of the risks posed by multiple natural hazards and the potential for mitigation and response approaches that take into account the interactions among different hazards and hazard vulnerabilities. It identifies risks in two ways: in a global multihazard analysis and in a set of hazard- or place-specific case studies.

Limitations of the global analysis include the following:

1. Global spatial data sets do not exist for the vulnerability characteristics of the major sets of elements at risk from each hazard, although in some cases vulnerability may be inferred from existing data on a limited basis.

2. Existing global spatial data sets on major hazards and elements at risk are of a coarse resolution, sufficient for resolving only relatively broad spatial patterns of risk.

3. Global data on socioeconomic "outcome" variables— such as mortality, morbidity, economic losses, and impoverishment—are universally available only at the country level, in the form of national statistics. However, such data are needed to verify the global risk assessment (that is, assessed spatial patterns of disaster risk hotspots should correspond to historical patterns of actual human and economic losses to some degree).

To partially address these limitations, case studies were undertaken to complement the global-scale analysis. The case studies use the same theory of disaster causality as the global analysis: that over a given time period, the risks of a specified type of disaster-related loss to a set of elements are a function of the elements'

exposure to natural hazards and their vulnerability to those hazards.

Two types of case studies were undertaken. One type examined the impacts of a particular hazard on a regional or global scale. Three such studies were performed, dealing with drought and disaster in Asia, global landslide risks, and storm surges in coastal areas.

The other type of study was geographically limited and identified risks associated with a particular hazard or combination of hazards using a richer set of location-specific data. These geographically limited case studies were designed to

1. "Ground truth" particular regions identified as potential hotspots;

2. Explore specific cases where more detailed loss probability data and models exist than are available globally;

3. Ascertain what finer scale data may exist locally, for example, on vulnerability, response capacity, and poverty;

4. Identify cross-hazard dependencies and interactions among hazards, exposure, vulnerability, and multihazard risk management;

5. Examine the policy context for risk management and the degree to which multiple hazards are recognized and addressed in an integrated manner;

6. Engage national- to local-level stakeholders; and

7. Demonstrate that the theory and methods that guide the global analysis can be applied on more regional or local geographic scales.

The three case studies in this category deal with multihazard risks in Sri Lanka; multihazard risks in Caracas, Venezuela; and flood risks in the Tana River Basin in Kenya.

Table 8.1 lists the six case studies and their authors.

Scale Issues

The place-based case studies demonstrate that scale matters. Geographic areas that are subsumed into a single hotspot at the global scale are shown to have a highly variable spatial distribution of risk at a more localized scale.

Scale also affects data availability and quality. Hazard, exposure, and vulnerability data are available at subnational resolutions for individual countries and even cities, as the analyses for Sri Lanka and Caracas show. More comprehensive, finer resolution, and better quality data contribute to more complete, accurate, and reliable risk assessments.

Better data resolution and a richer set of variables also contribute to results that are more relevant for national- to local-scale risk management planning. This is highly important, as decisions made at this level may have the greatest effect on risk levels, whether positively or negatively. In some instances, risk assessors and planners at the national and local levels may be able to "downscale" global data for larger scale risk assessment to compensate for a lack of locally collected data. In an ideal world, however, global analyses would be scaled up—generalized from more detailed local data. In practice, many barriers remain. Data sets may contain gaps, data for one country may not be available for a bordering country, and data on vulnerability characteristics for each hazard remain scanty. Vulnerability often must be inferred from proxies at best. The global infrastructure for systematically assembling and integrating relevant data sets for disaster risk assessment at multiple scales remains inadequate. Nonetheless, the fact that relevant data sets can be obtained at various scales and integrated for the case studies below creates the hope that one day data can be collected and shared routinely to improve disaster risk assessment both globally and locally.

Summary of Case Study Results

Hazard-focused, geographically extensive case studies

Drought Disaster in Asia

A drought disaster is caused by the combination of a climate hazard event (deficits in rain or snow) and societal vulnerability (the economic, social, and political characteristics that render livelihoods susceptible in affected areas). A pilot investigation for 27 countries in Asia compared the incidence of drought disasters recorded in EM-DAT with climatically defined drought hazard events.

Severe, persistent precipitation deficits as defined by the WASP index corresponded with reported drought

Table 8.1. Summary of Case Studies

Case Study	Contributors
Hazard-oriented	
Global Landslide and Avalanche Hotspots	Farrokh Nadim, Anne Sophie Gregoire, Carlos Rodriguez, Pascal Peduzzi, Oddvar Kjekstad
An Expert Assessment of Storm Surge "Hotspots"	Robert J. Nicholls
Toward Calculation of Global Drought Hazard: A Pilot Study for Asia	Matthew Barlow, Heidi Cullen, Brad Lyon, Olga Wilhelmi
Geographically focused	
Identification of Global Natural Disaster Risk Hotspots— Sri Lanka Case Study	Vidhura Ralapanawe, Lareef Zubair
Disaster Resilient Caracas	Kristina R. Czuchlewski, Klaus H. Jacob, Arthur L. Lerner-Lam, Kevin Vranes
Reducing the Impacts of Floods through Early Warning and Preparedness: A Pilot Study for Kenya	Hussein Gadain, Nicolas Bidault, Linda Stephen, Ben Watkins, Maxx Dilley, Nancy Mutunga

disasters most frequently in Asian countries with low average annual rainfall (Figure 8.1). In the 11 countries with annual precipitation less than 700 mm, drought disasters typically occurred 20 to 40 percent of the time in the three months following climatic drought events (defined as country-average 12-month WASP values of less than –1) from 1979 through 2001.

Widespread and prolonged precipitation deficits in the region from 1999 through 2001 were associated with drought disaster events among the countries in central southwest Asia, but not during the weaker but more prolonged dry period of the 1980s (Figure 8.2). In other parts of the region, the WASP threshold corresponded with disaster occurrence in both the 1980s and 1990s (see Lao People's Democratic Republic in Figure 8.3), while some countries are so large that a country average is not very meaningful (see India in Figure 8.3).

Varying degrees of correspondence between climatological drought events and drought disasters may be explained by two groups of factors. First, differences may be attributable to uneven reporting of disasters throughout the study period, uncertain precipitation data accuracy, and the choice of criteria for defining drought events. Second, differences may stem from the types of land uses and economic activities that were exposed to drought within the affected countries and their degree of vulnerability. Further research may clarify the combination of climatological and socio-economic factors that results in disaster. Such research could enhance the prospects for using data for real-time early warning of disasters.

Global Landslide Risks

This study performed a data-based, first-order identification of the geographic areas that constitute hotspots

Figure 8.1. Frequency with Which Climatic Drought Hazard Events Were Accompanied by Drought Disasters (Gold) or Not (Blue) from 1979 through 2001
Countries Have Been Ordered Left-To-Right Based on Annual Average Precipitation (Green Line, in millimeters).

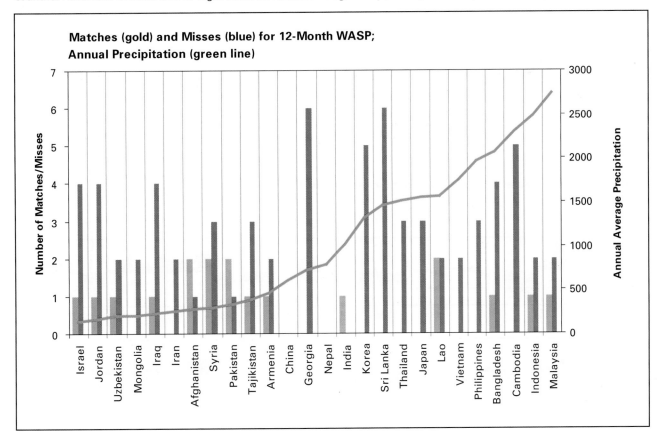

Figure 8.2. WASP Estimates of Climatic Drought (Shaded Brown Curve) and Drought Disasters (Red Bars) for Central Southwest Asian Ccountries

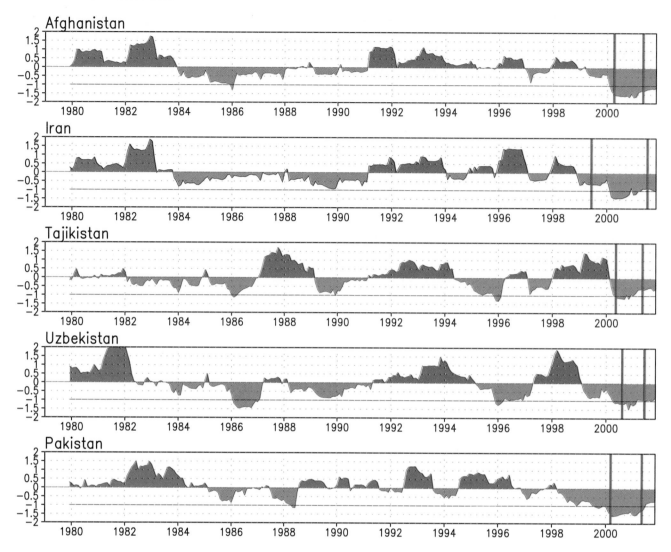

Figure 8.3. WASP Estimates of Climatic Drought (Shaded Brown Curve) and Drought Disasters (Red Bars) for Lao PDR and India

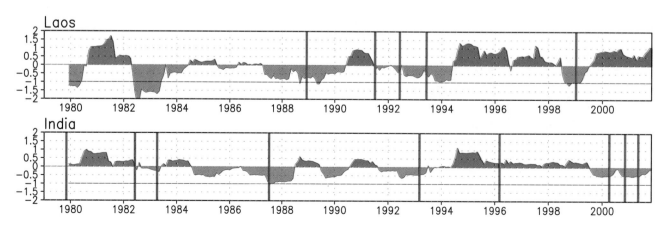

for global landslide disaster risk on a non-national scale, with an emphasis on developing countries. This identification includes combining landslide hazards with the vulnerability of people and infrastructure to obtain risks of losses.

The probability of landslides is estimated by modeling the physical processes combined with historical experience and statistics. Rapid mass movements such as rockslides, debris flows, and snow avalanches are included, whether triggered by precipitation or earthquakes. The main input data for assessing the landslide hazard are topography and slope angles, precipitation, seismic activity, soil type, hydrological condition, and vegetation. Snow avalanche probabilities are calculated from slope and relief, precipitation values from the winter months and temperature. The resulting combined global landslide and avalanche hazard map is an input to the global hotspots multihazard analysis described previously. The calculated landslide hazard corresponds well with historical data in selected case study areas (Figure 8.4).

Exposure and vulnerability derive from socioeconomic factors such as population density, quality of infrastructure, and response capacity. These factors were combined with the hazard estimates in an independent risk analysis calibrated with observed losses from the EM-DAT international disaster history database. The combination of gridded hazard probabilities (Figure 8.5) with exposure and vulnerability factors was used to calculate mortality risks (Figure 8.6).

Unlike the global risk analysis for landslides presented in Chapter 6, in this case vulnerability was characterized on the basis of national-level variables identified during the construction of the Disaster Risk Index (DRI) that provided the basis for the global risk assessment presented in *Reducing Disaster Risk: A Challenge for Development* (UNDP 2004). The case study companion volume to this report contains results of an analysis of global landslide risks prepared by the Norwegian Geotechnical Institute.

Storm Surges in Coastal Areas

Surges are positive or negative changes in sea level resulting from variations in atmospheric pressure and associated winds. They are additive to normal tides. When positive surges are added to high tides, they can cause extreme water levels and flooding. Surges are most commonly produced by the passage of atmospheric tropical or extratropical depressions. Positive surges can occur on any ocean coast, but they are best developed under extreme meteorological forcing and where the coastal morphology is favorable. Surges of two to three meters have been regularly observed in the southern North Sea, 6-meter surges are often associated with the landfall of a category 5 hurricane, and the largest surge ever observed was 13 meters, during a tropical cyclone in Australia. These surges are generally associated with strong wave activity, and the impacts of waves and surges need to be considered together.

Flooding caused by storm surges is a major hazard for coastal residents. In the past 200 years, at least 2.6 million people may have drowned because of storm surges, which also caused a range of other damage and disruption. Given that storms result in a number of hazards (surge/waves, winds, intense rainfall, tornadoes, and waterspouts), it is often quite difficult to isolate the specific impacts of the surge and hence attribute specific damage to surges. However, drowning by surge is the major killer in most coastal storms with high fatalities, so it is generally possible to link fatalities to surge events. This approach is followed in this case study.

The major impacts of surges are concentrated in a limited number of regions. Most fatalities in the past 200 years have occurred in Asia, especially around the Bay of Bengal, particularly in Bangladesh, where more than one million people may have died during the period (Murty 1984; Warrick and Ahmad 1996). This includes both the 1970 surge, when 300,000 to 500,000 people were killed and the 1991 surge, when about 140,000 people were killed. It is noteworthy that most of the surge events that have killed substantial numbers of people (over 10,000 deaths) have occurred where there have been substantial land claim and other human modifications to the coastal zone, suggesting that the hazard has coevolved with human modifications to the coastal zone. These areas include Bangladesh, China, Japan, and the southern North Sea. All of these areas have significantly adapted to the threat posed by surges. This adaptation is best developed around the North Sea and Japan, where surges have had very limited impacts since the 1960s, largely because of massive investment in flood defense infrastructure. Even in Bangladesh, improved

Figure 8.4. Modeled Landslide Zonation (Shading) and GEORISK Landslide Inventory (Blue) in Armenia

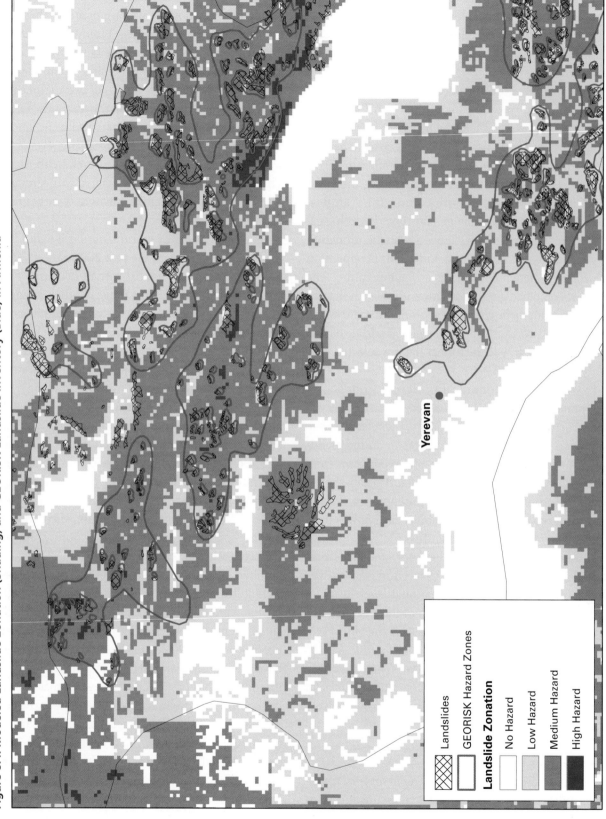

Yerevan

Landslides

GEORISK Hazard Zones

Landslide Zonation

No Hazard

Low Hazard

Medium Hazard

High Hazard

Figure 8.5. Landslide Hazard Map for Central America and Andean South America

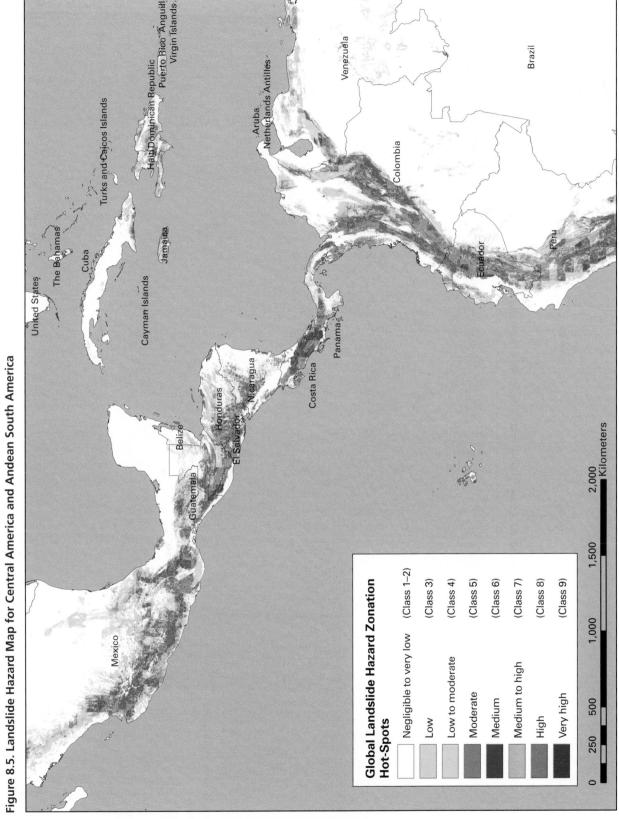

Global Landslide Hazard Zonation Hot-Spots

Negligible to very low	(Class 1–2)
Low	(Class 3)
Low to moderate	(Class 4)
Moderate	(Class 5)
Medium	(Class 6)
Medium to high	(Class 7)
High	(Class 8)
Very high	(Class 9)

Kilometers

0   250   500   1,000   1,500   2,000

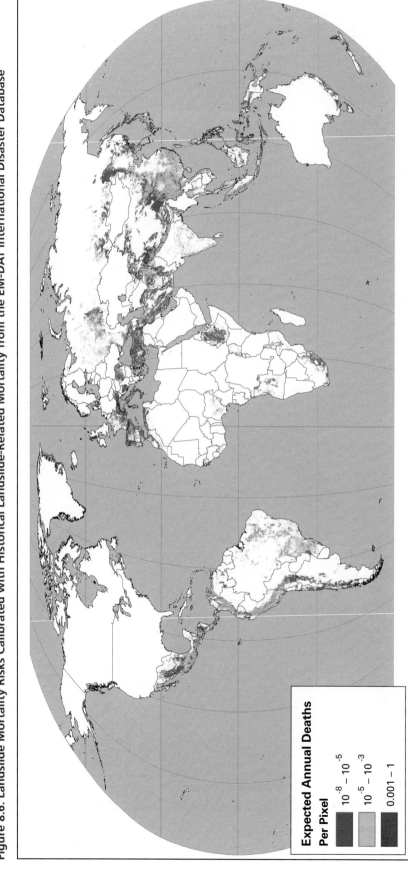

Figure 8.6. Landslide Mortality Risks Calibrated with Historical Landslide-Related Mortality from the EM-DAT International Disaster Database

Expected Annual Deaths Per Pixel

$10^{-8} - 10^{-5}$

$10^{-5} - 10^{-3}$

$0.001 - 1$

flood warnings appear to be reducing the number of fatalities significantly. However, there is no room for complacency. Even in the United States, with its highly effective storm warning systems, the potential for large numbers of fatalities remains (for example, a hurricane landfall on New Orleans or a major hurricane or northeaster impacting New York City).

The storm surge hazard will also continue to evolve as a result of socioeconomic and climate change, as well as continuing efforts to mitigate this hazard. Increased exposure in surge-prone areas may be problematic: areas such as eastern Africa that presently appear to have limited surge problems may see problems emerge if there is substantial population growth along the coast. Given that populated areas are particularly exposed, the likelihood of storm surge needs to be considered as these areas are developed.

The available data are not sufficient to define precise surge hotspots. It is most realistic to define the regions where major surge impacts might occur (see Table 8.2). Potential hotspots within these regions can then be identified on the basis of coastal elevation, coastal land use, and historical experience (as well as on the consideration of relevant scenarios).

Place-based case studies

Multihazard Risks in Sri Lanka
This case study exemplifies a high-resolution assessment of natural hazards, vulnerability to hazards, and disaster risk. Drought, flood, cyclone, and landslide hazards, as well as vulnerability to those hazards, were identified using data from Sri Lankan government agencies. Drought- and flood-prone areas were mapped using rainfall data that were gridded at a resolution of 10 kilometers. Cyclone and landslide hazards were mapped based on long-term historical incidence data. Indexes for regional industrial development, infrastructure development, and agricultural production were estimated on the basis of proxies. An assessment of regional food insecurity from the World Food Programme was used in the analysis. Records of emergency relief were used in estimating a spatial proxy for disaster risk. A multihazard map was developed for Sri Lanka based on the estimates of regional drought, flood, cyclone, and landslide hazards. The hazard estimates for drought, floods, cyclones,

and landslides were weighted for their associated disaster risk with proxies for economic losses to provide a risk map or a hotspots map. Principal findings include the following:

1. Useful hazard and vulnerability analysis can be carried out with the type of data that is available in-country. The hazard estimates for droughts, floods, cyclones, and landslides show marked spatial variability. Vulnerability shows marked spatial variability as well. Thus, the resolution of analysis needs to match the resolution of spatial variations in relief, climate, and other features. Analyses of disasters need higher spatial and temporal resolution for planning and action at the local level.

2. Multihazard analysis brought out regions of high risk such as the Kegalle and Ratnapura districts in the southwest; the Ampara, Batticaloa, Trincomalee, Mullaitivu, and Killinochchi districts in the northeast; and the districts of Nuwara Eliya, Badulla, Ampara, and Matale, which contain some of the sharpest hill slopes of the central mountain massifs.

3. There is a distinct seasonality to risks posed by drought, floods, landslides, and cyclones. Whereas the eastern regions have hotspots during the boreal fall and early winter, the western-slopes regions are risk prone in the summer and the early fall. Thus, attention is warranted not only on hotspots but also on "hot seasons."

4. Climate data were useful for estimating the degree of hazard in the case of droughts, floods, and cyclones and the risk of flood and landslide. The methodologies used here for hazard analysis of floods and droughts present an explicit link between climate and hazard. This link can be used in conjunction with seasonal climate prediction to provide predictive hazard risk estimates in the future.

5. Climatic, environmental, and social changes such as deforestation, urbanization, and war affect hazard exposure and vulnerability. It is more difficult to quantify such changes than the baseline conditions. However, climate change is already making parts of the island more prone to drought hazard.

Table 8.2. An Expert Synthesis of Storm Surge Hotspots around the World

Surge-Prone Regions	Hotspots		Commentary
	*Fatalities**	*Other Damage*	
Bay of Bengal (Bangladesh and Eastern India)	High	High	Improved flood warnings may reduce fatalities
Western India/Pakistan	Unclear	Unclear	Cyclones are less frequent than Bay of Bengal (1:4) and there is less exposure
China/Japan	Potentially high	Potentially high	Ongoing flood damage is reported in China
Korea, Rep. of	Low	Low	Region lacks large low-lying coastal areas, but this is changing owing to extensive land claim
Thailand, Vietnam, Philippines	Potentially high in deltas	Medium to high	Region is frequently impacted by typhoons, and population of low-lying areas is growing rapidly
Pacific Islands	Probably high	High	Limited historical information
Australia and New Zealand	Low	Low	Region has limited habitation in low-lying coastal areas
Indian Ocean Islands	Low	Low	Region has limited habitation in low-lying coastal areas
Eastern Africa and Oman	Low	Low	Habitation in low-lying coastal areas is not significant, but could increase
Rio de la Plata (Argentina and Uruguay)	Low	Low	Difficult to assess, owing to limited literature—may suggest limited impacts to date
Caribbean	Potentially high	Medium to high	Human activity is concentrated around the islands, and hence exposed to surge. However, the role of surge relative to other hurricane impacts is less clear
Central America and Mexico	Potentially high in local areas	Medium to high	Human activity is often concentrated away from the coast, which is atypical at the global level. Hence other hurricane impacts appear more important than in other regions (for example, Hurricane Mitch), although there are localized hotspots.
United States—Gulf and East coasts	Potentially high	High	Effective evacuation has reduced fatalities, but potential hotspots remain
Europe—Atlantic coast	Potentially high	Potentially high	Hard defenses and improved flood predictions and warnings appear to have been effective in reducing this hazard
Europe—Mediterranean coast	Locally high	Medium to high	Surges are not large, so deaths are unlikely, except in areas of land claim where flood depths could be substantial. However, significant damage and disruption can occur.
Europe—North Sea coast	Potentially high	Potentially high	Hard defenses and improved flood predictions and warnings appear to have been effective in reducing this hazard
Europe—Baltic Sea coast	Locally high	Medium to high	Hard defenses and improved flood predictions and warnings appear to have been effective in reducing this hazard

* In the column titled "Fatalities," "high" indicates the potential for more than 1,000 deaths in a surge event. Other damage estimates are based on the expert judgment of the author.

6. The analysis was carried out in the context of civil wars from 1983 to 2002. While natural disasters accounted for 1,483 fatalities in this period, civil wars accounted for more than 65,000. Wars and conflict complicate natural hazard and vulnerability analysis. However, the vulnerabilities created by the war make efforts to reduce disaster risks all the more important.

Risks are calculated in a number of different ways, and several alternative multihazard risk maps are presented. Subject to data limitations, records of past disasters are used to weight for exposure and vulnerability to particular hazards.

One multihazard map is generated by weighting hazard frequency with historical disasters obtained from the EM-DAT database (Figure 8.7). Multiple landslides within a single year were treated as one event.

Another multihazard risk map was calculated by weighting each hazard index by the disaster relief expenditure data from the Sri Lanka Department of Social Services for each hazard (Figure 8.8). This resulting map is heavily weighted toward droughts and cyclones, with landslides receiving a meager weight.

This hotspots map shows higher risk in the north and north central regions and in Hambantota District in the southeast compared with the previous map. Determining which methodology to employ will be based in part on considerations regarding the application of the analysis for risk management.

Determining which methodology to employ will be based in part on considerations regarding the application of the analysis for risk management.

Weights based on relief expenditures obtained from the Sri Lanka Department of Social Services: Drought: 126, Floods: 25, Landslides: 0.06, Cyclones: 60. The weighted index has been rescaled to the range 0 to 100.

Multihazard Risks in Caracas, Venezuela

Cities are centers of economic opportunity and culture, and are a natural focus for investment and development. The role of cities is recognized globally in the trend toward increasing urbanization in most countries. However, the increased concentration of physical and cultural assets that accompanies increases in the spatial density of population also increases their exposure to geographically limited natural hazards. If these assets are fragile (vulnerable), then the city is at risk. A region or country that depends on the sustainable growth of its cities shares the risk. Risk management for existing and developing metropolitan areas is thus a component of development policy.

This report summarizes the findings of a preliminary study of the natural hazards faced by Caracas, Venezuela, and proposes ways in which urban planning and design can incorporate a qualitative natural hazards risk assessment. The report is designed to be illustrative rather than comprehensive, since the development of an urban plan is a complicated and organic task with many stakeholders. However, the methodological approach described in this work can serve as the basis for such a plan and be applied to other cities and regions.

Located on the intersection of the South American and Caribbean Plates, northern Venezuela faces extreme seismological hazards. Major earthquakes have destroyed Caracas three times in the last 400 years. The last large earthquake (Mw = 6.5) came in 1967, killing an estimated 300 people and destroying four modern structures built for earthquake resistance (Papageorgiou and Kim 1991). In addition, the position of the northern coast near 10°N ensures frequent heavy rainfall events with strong erosion potential. In December 1999, a month of rain on the north central coast of Venezuela—including over 900 millimeters of rain in a 72-hour period between 15 and 17 December—triggered landslides, mudflows, and debris flows on the north face of the El Ávila range that killed an estimated 25,000 residents of the coastal state of Vargas.

Since the last major earthquake in 1967, the population of Caracas has doubled to five million people, with a population density of 12,000 persons per square kilometer and growth of 3.1 percent per year. Eighty-six percent of the Venezuelan population is urban, making it the seventh most urbanized country in the world. The valley floor is well developed, with high-rise buildings and densely packed apartment blocks scattered unevenly throughout the city. These buildings are generally concentrated in the deepest part of the basin (where shaking is expected to be highest during an earthquake).

Barrios, or informal squatter settlements, dominate the landscape on the low-lying, rugged mountains to the east and west of the city center, where rainfall-induced

Figure 8.7 Multihazard Risk Map Constructed by Weighting Each Hazard Index by Incidence Frequency Data from EM-DAT Database

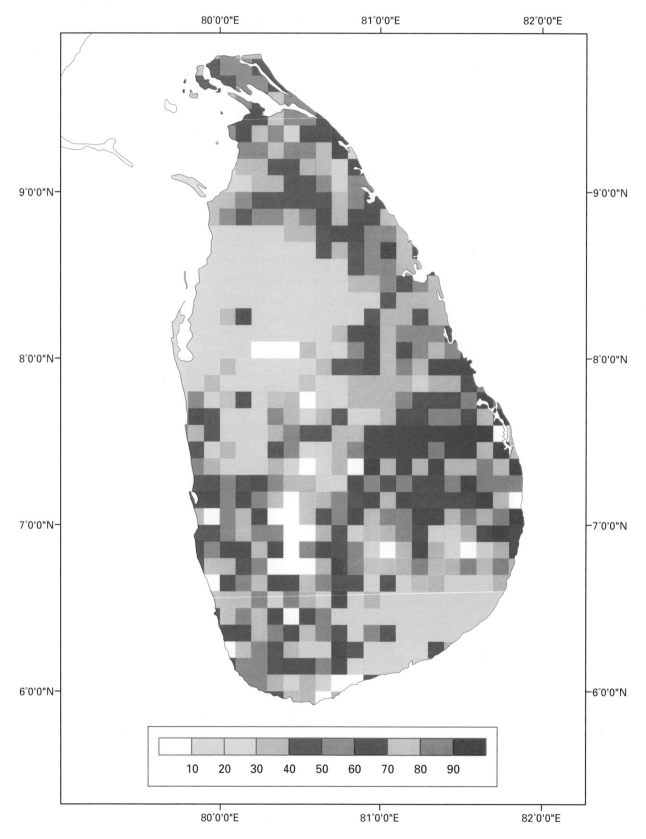

Figure 8.8 Multihazard Risk Map Constructed by Weighting Each Hazard Index by the Relief Expenditure Data for Each Hazard Between 1948 and 1992

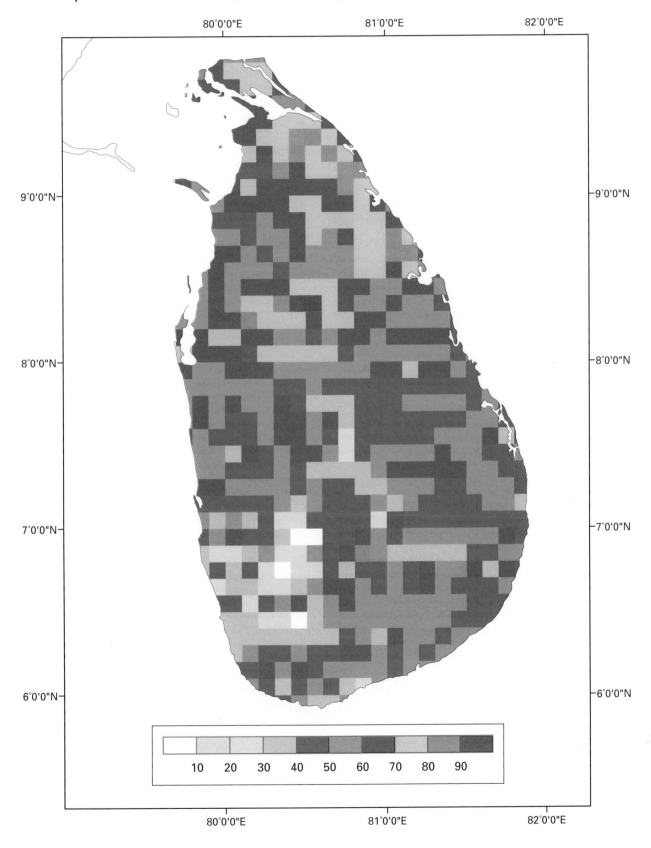

debris flows are expected to be greatest. To the south is a mixture of *urbanizaciónes* (similar to suburbs) and *barrios*. The individual building blocks of the *barrios*, known as *ranchos*, are constructed of unreinforced masonry, making them particularly vulnerable to earthquakes.

Centuries ago, Caracas was purposefully built away from the coast and through steep terrain to deter seaborne attacks on the city. However, this removal creates major transportation and utility infrastructure problems that are exacerbated by natural hazards. Caracas is linked to the world through its airport and seaport, both of which are located across El Ávila on the Vargas coast. The only road between Caracas and the airport and seaport is a highway that travels through steep, landslide-prone valleys crossing secondary faults that are part of the active San Sebastian fault system.

Uncontrolled building and unenforced building and zoning codes in this hazardous environment have led to human disasters and potential problems of great magnitude. A lack of building codes and their enforcement allowed Vargas residents to build on active (but quiescent for the previous 50 years) alluvial fans, which reactivated during December 1999. Although various groups are working to repair and rebuild Vargas State with new housing built in safe locations, poor planning and code enforcement are allowing squatters to return to the alluvial fans and streambeds where most of the December 1999 destruction was concentrated.

Seismic, landslide, and flood hazards affect a high proportion of Caracas's urban infrastructure, including housing (Figure 8.9). The case study explores aspects of risk management based on the risks identified.

Flood Risk Assessment for Contingency Planning in the Lower Tana River Basin, Kenya

Many Sub-Saharan African countries experience extreme weather conditions leading to severe flood events that require humanitarian assistance. Emergency preparedness is a prerequisite for humanitarian response to be effective, coordinated, dependable, and timely. A critical factor that has hampered responding agencies in many countries is lack of information on who will be affected and what impacts are expected.

This case study uses a streamflow model and flood hazard mapping to generate flood scenarios for the lower Tana River Basin, a flood-prone area in Kenya where emergency assistance is frequently required (Figure 8.10). Flood risks to the population and livelihoods are assessed using a livelihood zonation data set that includes populated places. Flood inundation maps associated with the river depths for the 1961 and El Niño-related floods in 1997–98 were generated, and impacts assessed for moderate and severe flood event scenarios. The results are interpreted for use in contingency planning and preparedness.

The Tana River District in the coast province is divided into seven administrative divisions with a total area of 38,694 square kilometers. The topography, drainage pattern, and soil determine the large extent of the intense flooding. The district is generally an undulating plain, which slopes southeast with an altitude ranging between 0.0 and 200 meters above sea level. The main physical geographical feature of this district is the Tana River. The large floodbasin, whose width ranges from 2 to 40 kilometers, provides fertile arable land and is the economic backbone of the district. The hinterland has seasonal streams (*lagas*), which provide wet-season grazing areas and are sources of inlets for earth pans. Soils in Tana River district are divided into two groups: well-drained sandy soils ranging in color from white to red, and poorly drained silty and clayey soils that are gray and black in color.

Nomadic pastoralists who keep large herds of cattle, goats, and sheep mainly occupy the hinterland. In 1997, during a three-month period, the district received over 1,200 millimeters of El Niño-related rainfall, triple its annual average. The resulting floods destroyed many houses, damaged infrastructure, swept away crops, and killed livestock.

Garissa district is one of three districts that make up the North Eastern Province of Kenya. The total population of the district is 231,000, according to 1999 census population projections. About 40 percent of the population resides within Garissa town. The district is predominately inhabited by Somali people who traditionally practice livestock keeping.

The climate of Garissa is semiarid, and the long-term average rainfall is about 300 mm. Prior to the 1997–98 El Niño rains, the greatest rainfall occurred in 1961 and 1968, when an average of 920 millimeters was measured at many stations. Unusually heavy rains in 1997

Figure 8.9. Multihazard disaster risk, Caracas.

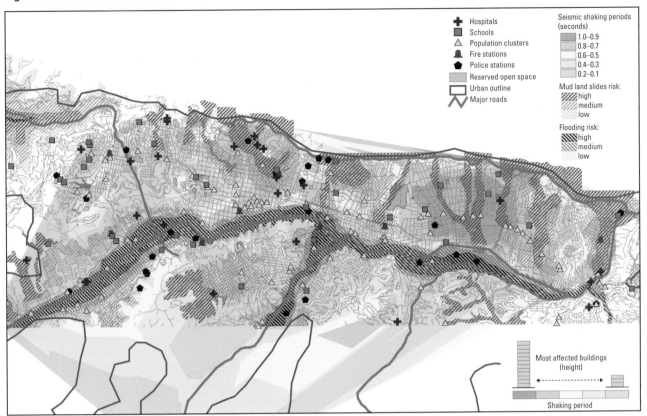

totaled 1,027 millimeters; 925 millimeters occurred between October and December 1997. This was a huge amount of rainfall for an area receiving an annual average of 300 millimeters.

This case study assessed risks of worst-case flood impacts on livelihoods using the El Niño flooding event of 1997–98, with an estimated 35-year return period as a scenario. The impact of floods on populations differs depending on their livelihoods and wealth group. Among the different livelihood groups in both districts, the ones most exposed to flooding are pastoralists, agro-pastoralists, and the dry riverine and Tana Delta livelihood systems (Figure 8.11).

The livelihood zones directly on the river (dry riverine zone, Tana Delta zone, pastoralist, and agro-pastoralist—the latter mostly located in the hinterland, except in the south part of the basin) are likely to be impacted by the direct destruction of their properties (such as houses, crop fields, and pumps). The population in the urban area (especially at Garissa town) is likely to be mostly affected through the indirect

effect of the floods, such as an interruption of access to markets and concomitant loss of income, though some may also lose property. However, people in urban areas are more likely to have resources to cope and therefore are less at risk of complete collapse of their livelihood. The population in fisheries and subsistence cropping may find benefits in the floods, thanks to the likely increase in fish production, but they are also likely to see their subsistence cropping resources affected.

Cash income for the pastoralist community is not diversified at all, as 68 percent of total cash income comes from livestock. This is also the case for agro-pastoralists, 40 percent of whose income comes from livestock. To a lesser extent, people in the dry riverine zone also derive much of their income from livestock (22 percent). During the El Niño floods of 1997–98, close to 90 percent of sheep and goats died in the Garissa and Tana River districts, resulting in complete collapse of that source of income. For these three groups, sheep and goats represent close to 15 percent of their total income. In addition, for larger animals, which were less directly

Figure 8.10. Location Map of Tana River and Garissa Districts with Coverage of Tana River Basin in Garissa District, Kenya

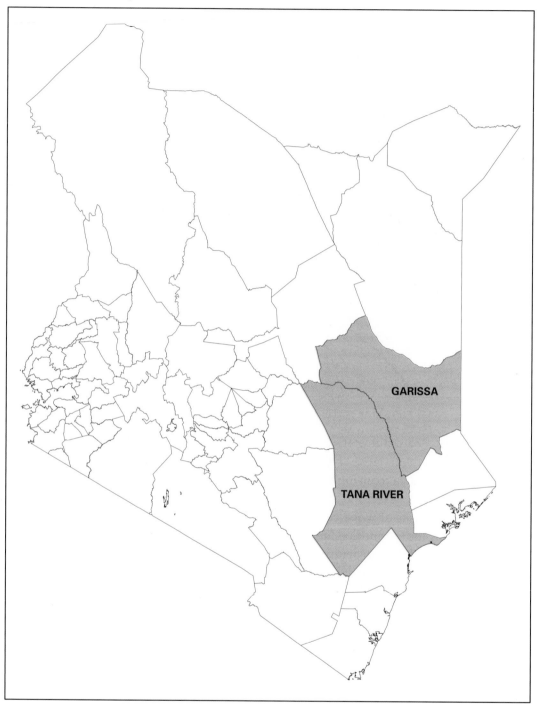

Figure 8.11. Livelihood Zones Overlaid on El Niño 1997–98 Flood Case (Estimated Return Period 35 years)

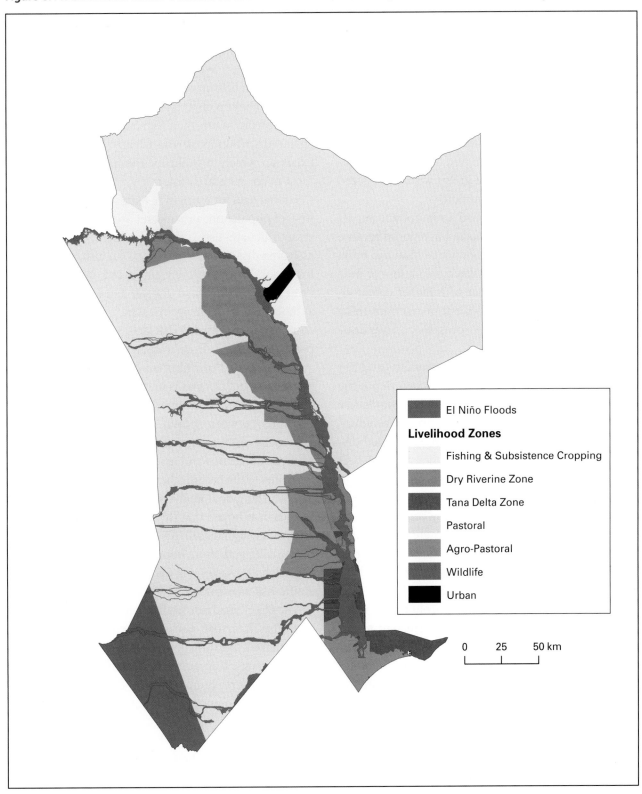

affected by floods, mortality and morbidity increased dramatically as a result of diseases such as foot rot and pneumonia. In addition to the direct loss of animals, the decrease in livestock marketability also hurt income. Because of the fear of Rift Valley fever, animals were not bought on the markets and income from animal sales was lost. The impact on livestock has hurt equally the "very poor," "poor," and "middle" groups, who have seen their income from livestock reduced to zero. Most of the very poor and poor have moved to the destitute category, while only the middle group with larger-sized cattle may have avoided destitution.

The loss of livestock also had an important impact on food consumption. Food intake was reduced because of the loss of animals that had provided meat and milk. The loss of income also translated into a loss of purchasing power, which together with higher commodity prices put the commodities out of reach for these communities. As a result, their access to food was drastically reduced.

Under the worst case scenario, pastoralists and dry riverine communities are expected to experience the worst losses. Therefore, a response directed toward these groups, particularly the pastoralists, would be advisable. Assistance should take the form of free food distribution and income-generating activities, as the analysis has shown that for all of the groups, income, daily food consumption, and nutrition are tied to livestock and crop production, both of which may completely collapse in any flood scenario. Furthermore, assessments during the 1997–98 El Niño floods showed that relief food enabled pastoralists to save their remaining livestock and to start rebuilding herds and livelihoods. For planning purposes, we know from our hazard maps that food assistance in the short term and income regenerating activities in the long term would be required for up to 70,000 persons. In a moderate-case scenario, the population in need would be 47,000. This finding provides core data for calculating the volume of food commodities required and costs.

Linkages to and Lessons for Global Analysis

The global Hotspots analysis is intended as a first-order filter to reveal areas of highest disaster risk from one or multiple hazards. To accomplish this, several hazard databases had to be created or substantially strengthened. Two of these—droughts and landslides (floods being the third)—are explored in case studies in this chapter. Work to improve hazard data must continue. While storm surges are not incorporated directly into the global Hotspots analysis, the case study here illustrates both their damaging potential and the spatial distribution of risk. Clearly an adequate base exists on which to build for the hazards involved in most major natural disasters.

Global data for estimating exposure and vulnerability—of population, agriculture, urban areas, and infrastructure—are also sufficiently developed for use in assessing disaster risks. Data sets on historical disaster losses are being explored, improved, and integrated. Over time, accumulated disaster and loss data provide a dependent variable against which the contributions of independent variable risk factors to spatial and temporal variations in losses can be calculated.

One intended contribution of the multiscale nature of the hotspots analysis is to demonstrate the transferability of disaster causality theory and risk assessment methods between spatial scales. The same general approach—estimating exposure of elements at risk to an array of hazards and assessing their degrees of vulnerability to the hazards they face—has been employed in both the global analysis and the place-based case studies. It is hoped that the durability and rigor of the approach will lend itself to a continuing effort to improve data quality and, more important, to a more systematic approach to disaster risk management founded on scientific risk assessment.

The place-based case studies demonstrate how second- and third-order risk assessments can be conducted in areas that include hotspots identified by the first-order global analysis. This multitiered approach creates opportunities to achieve appropriate data density within hotspots for a more precise analysis of risks and their causal factors.

The case studies, both hazard-focused and place-based, also illustrate how single and multiple hazards interact with exposed elements and their vulnerabilities to create complex patterns of risk. These interactions among causal factors of disaster are an important topic for continuing research. The case studies suggest that multihazard phenomena observed at coarse resolution on global scales may lead to multihazard management problems at national and urban scales of analysis and decision making. Given resource constraints and the multiple roles played by key infrastructure such as roads, railroads, and ports in disaster preparedness, emergency response, reconstruction, and ongoing economic activity, it is vital that planners and decision makers at all levels understand the hazards prevalent in their own regions. In particular, they need to understand the potential interactions among these hazards, whether direct (such as storms that trigger both floods and landslides) or indirect (such as consecutive hazard events that strain response capacities and exacerbate vulnerabilities).

The combination of global and national or local-scale analyses based on common theory, methods, and, in some cases, data provides opportunities to integrate risk management strategies at multiple scales toward a common objective of reducing disaster losses. Through these analyses, international donors operating at the global scale, for example, can focus attention and resources on high-risk regions. National and local authorities can use similar techniques to formulate proactive and effective risk management plans that target verifiable risks transparently and objectively. Global/national partnerships to reduce risks in highest risk areas may be the only way for some disaster-prone countries to stem the tide of disaster losses that impede their social and economic development. Focusing on risk management rather than disaster relief would greatly benefit some countries, cut costs for donors, and free up resources for promoting positive development.

Another factor that emerged in several of the case studies was the importance of temporal variations in risk. Now that the initial global risk assessment is complete and the case studies have demonstrated the usefulness of the theory to local risk assessment, a temporal dimension can be added. This dimension should be added to monitoring and forecasting risk levels, especially in the highest risk, most disaster-prone areas. This dimension is particularly critical for hazards for which early warning is currently possible: droughts, floods, cyclones, and volcanoes, as well as some landslides. Cutting-edge work on hazard event prediction, particularly if combined with more systematic exposure and vulnerability monitoring, could improve disaster early warning on a temporal basis, with an emphasis on early warning systems in high-risk areas.

As important as the incremental improvement in risk assessment is fostering and promoting the ability to use information about risks effectively for risk reduction and transfer. This application of the results of risk identification is explored in the Caracas and Tana River case studies. The underlying rationale for risk assessment is that it reveals where investments in risk reduction are most needed and likely to have the biggest payoff in terms of reduced losses. Much remains to be learned, however, about how to use this type of information to best advantage, including the institutions, policies, cost/benefit analyses, mitigation measures, and resource allocation decisions needed to convert risk information to disaster reduction. It is important that this type of work be integrated into efforts to improve risk assessment and vice versa.

Quantitative data-based risk assessment, combined with successful efforts to reduce risks, creates greater potential for risk transfer through insurance and other mechanisms. These offer the opportunity for populations at risk to transfer some of the risk to a wider base of risk-holders. While disaster risk will never be eliminated, an approach that combines risk identification, reduction, and transfer offers the best possibility of minimizing losses and repeated and expensive relief and reconstruction efforts.

Table 8.3. Potential and Actual Hotspots Vulnerable to Flooding by Storm Surge*

Surge-Prone Regions	*Potential and Actual Hotspots*
Bay of Bengal (Bangladesh and Eastern India)	Ganges-Brahmaputra mouth (Bangladesh and West Bengal); Mahandi delta (Orissa); and the Krishna and Godavari deltas (Andhra Pradesh)
Western India/Pakistan	Indus delta and Karachi (Pakistan); Mumbai (India)
China/Japan	Lower Liaohe River Plain (China); North China Plain (China); East China Plain and Shanghai (China); Hanjiang River deltiac plain (China); Pearl River deltaic plain; Guangzhou and Hong Kong (China); Guangxi coastal plain (China); North Hainan Plain (China); Taiwan (China) coastal plain; Taipei (Taiwan, China); Metropolitan Toyko (Japan); Metropolitan Osaka (Japan)
Korea, Rep. of	—
Thailand, Vietnam, Philippines	Red River delta (Vietnam); Mekong delta (Vietnam); Metropolitan Manila (Philippines); Chaophraya delta and Bangkok (Thailand)
Pacific Islands	Most capital cities, all of which are on the coast; all atoll islands
Australia and New Zealand	—
Indian Ocean Islands	—
Eastern Africa and Oman	—
Rio de la Plata (Argentina and Uruguay)	Buenos Aires (Argentina); Montevideo (Uruguay)
Caribbean	Most capital cities, all of which are on the coast
Central America and Mexico	—
United States—Gulf and East coasts	New York City; Florida, particularly southern Florida and the Keys; New Orleans
Europe—Atlantic coast	—
Europe—Mediterranean coast	Areas of land claim and high subsidence on the Northern Adriatic Coastal Plain in Italy (Nicholls and Hoozemans 1996)
Europe—North Sea coast	London and Kingston-upon-Hull (United Kingdom); the western Netherlands; Hamburg and Bremen (Germany)
Europe—Baltic Sea coast	St. Petersburg (Russia); potentially Helsinki (Finland) and Stockholm (Sweden)

* This information is indicative rather than an exhaustive list of potential and actual hotspots.

Note: — none

Chapter 9
Conclusions and the Way Forward

This project has made a unique attempt to develop a global, synoptic view of the major natural hazards, assessing risks of multiple disaster-related outcomes and focusing in particular on the degree of overlap between areas exposed to multiple hazards. This exploratory effort has used a range of existing and recently developed data sets to create an initial picture of the location and characteristics of hotspots: areas at relatively high risk from one or more natural hazards. Although many researchers have justifiably critiqued the quality of these data for detailed quantitative analysis of the risks posed by natural hazards, the data do permit differentiation of areas of relatively high hazard from areas of lower hazard. Combining these data across hazards using simple categorical methods thus enables objective identification of hotspots.

The study also undertook a range of case studies designed to provide important insights into the Hotspots analysis, to test the applicability of the approach at subglobal scales, and to explore the value of understanding multihazard interactions at subnational scales.

The Costs of Disaster Risks

The combination of human and economic losses, plus the additional costs of relief, rehabilitation, and reconstruction, makes disasters an economic as well as a humanitarian issue. Until vulnerability, and consequently risks, are reduced, countries with high proportions of population or GDP in hotspots are especially likely to incur repeated disaster-related losses and costs. Disaster risks, therefore, deserve serious consideration as an issue for sustainable development.

The significance of high mortality and economic loss risks for socioeconomic development indicated in this analysis extends well beyond the initial direct losses to the population and economy during disasters. Covariate losses accompanying mortality, for example, include partial or total loss of household assets, lost income, and lost productivity. Widespread disaster-related mortality can affect households and communities for years, decades, and even generations.

In addition to mortality and its long-term consequences, both direct and indirect economic losses must be considered (ECLAC and the World Bank 2003). Direct losses are losses of assets, whereas indirect losses are the losses that accrue while productive assets remain damaged or destroyed. During disasters, both direct and indirect losses accumulate across the social, productive, and infrastructure sectors. The pattern of losses depends on the type of hazard and the affected sectors' vulnerabilities to the hazard. In large disasters, cumulative losses across sectors can have macroeconomic impacts.

Disasters impose costs in addition to human and economic losses. Additional costs include expenditures for disaster relief and recovery and for rehabilitation and reconstruction of damaged and destroyed assets. In major disasters, meeting these additional costs can require external financing or international humanitarian assistance.

Data on relief costs associated with natural disasters are available from the Financial Tracking System (FTS) of the United Nations Office for the Coordination of Humanitarian Affairs (OCHA) for 1992 through 2003. The FTS database contains information on all humanitarian aid contributions as reported to OCHA by international donors (http://www.reliefweb.int/fts/). Total relief costs for 1992 through 2003 are US$2.5

Table 9.1. Countries Receiving High Levels of International Disaster Assistance, 1992 through 2003

Country	Earthquakes	Floods	Storms	Drought	Volcanoes
China	X	X			
India	X	X	X		
Bangladesh		X			
Egypt, Arab Rep.	X				
Mozambique		X			
Turkey	X				
Afghanistan	X			X	
El Salvador	X				
Kenya		X		X	
Iran, the Islamic Rep. of	X				
Pakistan		X		X	
Indonesia	X	X		X	
Peru	X	X			
Congo, Dem. Rep. of					X
Poland		X			
Vietnam		X	X		
Colombia	X				
Venezuela		X			
Tajikistan		X		X	
Cambodia		X			

Source: OCHA.

billion. Of this, $2 billion went to just 20 countries (Table 9.1).

The World Bank provided data for this study on emergency loans and reallocation of existing loans to meet disaster reconstruction needs for 1980 through 2003 (http://www.worldbank.org/hazards). The total emergency lending and loan reallocation for 1980 through 2003 was US$14.4 billion. Of this, $12 billion went to the top 20 countries (Table 9.2).

High proportions of the population, GDP per unit area, or land surface area in the countries listed in Tables 9.1 and 9.2 fall within areas identified above as high-risk hotspots. Presumably, as disasters continue to occur, these and other high-risk countries will continue to need high levels of humanitarian relief and recovery lending unless their vulnerability is reduced.

Disaster relief costs drain development resources from productive investments to support consumption over short periods. Emergency loans have questionable value as vehicles for long-term investment and contribute to country indebtedness without necessarily improving economic growth or reducing poverty.

The most significant implications of having large numbers of people, GDP, or land surface at risk can be seen in profiles of economic losses from six illustrative disasters in which losses were assessed using a stan-

dardized comprehensive methodology (ECLAC and the World Bank 2003). The assessment method allows losses to be disaggregated by sector and into direct asset losses as well as into indirect losses due to the loss of productive assets. A look at losses by sector and hazard type for these six disasters clarifies the financial implications of future losses for the hotspots and suggests what the actual losses might have been in thousands of past disasters for which comprehensive assessments were not conducted.[3]

Total direct and indirect losses for six major disasters were obtained from the Economic Commission for Latin America and the Caribbean (ECLAC) and the World Bank. These disasters were earthquakes in Turkey in 1999 and in India and El Salvador in 2001; Hurricane Keith in Belize in 2000; the Mozambique floods in 2000; and a drought in Central America in 2001 (Table 9.3). The total direct and indirect loss for these six disasters alone was US$9.5 billion. Relief costs (OCHA) and reconstruction loans (World Bank) totaled $487.4 million and

---

[3] Due to the fact that data from comprehensive assessments of direct and indirect economic losses have not been systematically compiled and reported to date, economic loss estimates in EM-DAT, where they exist, are based on ad hoc reporting.

Table 9.2. Countries Receiving Emergency Loans and Reallocation of Existing Loans to Meet Disaster Reconstruction Needs, 1980 through 2003

Country	Earthquakes	Floods	Storms	Drought	Volcanoes
India	X		X	X	
Turkey	X	X			
Bangladesh		X	X		
Mexico	X	X			
Argentina		X			
Brazil		X			
Poland		X			
Colombia	X	X			
Iran, the Islamic Rep. of	X				
Honduras		X	X		
China	X	X			
Chile	X				
Zimbabwe				X	
Dominican Republic			X		
El Salvador	X				
Algeria	X	X			
Ecuador	X	X			
Mozambique		X		X	
Philippines	X				
Vietnam		X			

Source: World Bank Hazard Management Unit (http://www.worldbank.org/hazards).

$1.4 billion, respectively—5 percent and 14 percent, respectively, of the total estimated loss.

Neither the OCHA relief costs nor the World Bank reconstruction loan figures necessarily fully account for the total relief and reconstruction expenditures in these six disasters. Nevertheless, the above figures, where data on all three variables are available, suggest that economic losses across all sectors in disasters may considerably exceed the costs of relief and reconstruction. Thus, the greatest financial implications for the hotspot areas may be with respect to potential future economic losses.

Hazards are not the cause of disasters. By definition, disasters involve large human or economic losses. Hazard events that occur in unpopulated areas and are not associated with losses do not constitute disasters. Losses are created not only by hazards, therefore, but also by the intrinsic characteristics of the exposed infrastructure, land uses, and economic activities that cause them to be damaged or destroyed when a hazard strikes. This socioeconomic contribution to disaster causality is potentially a source of disaster reduction. Disaster losses can be reduced by reducing exposure or vulnerability to the hazards present in a given area.

Implications for Decision Making

The Hotspots analysis has implications for development investment planning, disaster preparedness and loss prevention. The highest risk areas are those in which disasters are expected to occur most frequently and losses are expected to be highest. This provides a rational basis for prioritizing risk-reduction efforts and highlights areas where risk management is most needed.

For preparedness, identification of high-risk areas provides a basis for contingency planning. The global analysis is appropriate for identifying which types of hazards affect which parts of countries and groups of countries. This allows international relief organizations to anticipate what types of problems might occur, and where, and plan accordingly.

For preventing losses, risk identification paves the way for risk reduction and risk transfer. Currently, risks are so high in some areas that they are uninsurable. Reducing them could create opportunities for at-risk populations or countries to sell part of their risk instead of bearing it all themselves.

The resolution of the global data is most appropriate for only very general types of international-scale

Table 9.3 Direct and Indirect Losses for Six Major Disasters

Hazard	Year	Country	Social Sectors (10^6 US$)	Infrastructure Sectors (10^6 US$)	Productive Sectors (10^6 US$)	Environment and Other (10^6 US$)	Total (10^6 US$)
Earthquake	1999	Turkey (Marmara)	2,187	739	1,850	0	4,776
Earthquake	2001	India (Gujarat)	1,302	334	440	55	2,131
Earthquake	2001	El Salvador	472	398	275	68	1,212
Hurricane	2000	Belize	38	44	165	407	655
Flood	2000	Mozambique	69	133	281	5	488
Drought	2001	Central America	124	3	83	0	210
Total			4,191	1,651	3,095	535	9,472

Sources: ECLAC and the World Bank.

decision making, however, and the global map indicates the need for more localized work with better data. In particular, more localized work allows greater specificity in identifying vulnerability factors, which identify the greatest opportunities for risk reduction. As the previous chapters have shown, the methods used for assessing risks globally can be used for work at the national and local levels.

International development organizations are key stakeholders with respect to the global analysis. The analysis provides a scientific basis for understanding where risks are highest and why, as well as a methodological framework for regional- and local-scale analysis. The identified risks then can be evaluated further using more detailed data in the context of a region's or country's overall development strategy and priorities. This would serve development institutions and the countries in several ways to facilitate the development of better-informed investment strategies and activities.

Assistance Strategies. So for example, a development institution such as the World Bank may use the analysis at the global and/or regional level to identify countries that are at higher risk for disasters and "flag" them as priorities to ensure that disaster risk management is addressed in the development of a Country Assistance Strategy (CAS) or Poverty Reduction Strategy.

While in some countries there can be a seemingly long list of urgent priorities to address in a CAS—e.g., reducing extreme poverty, fighting HIV/AIDS, promoting education, achieving macroeconomic stability—managing disaster risk should be considered an integral part of the development planning to protect the investments made, rather than as a stand-alone agenda. The CAS should consider the consequences of unmitigated

disaster risk in terms of possible tradeoffs with long-term socioeconomic goals.

In high-risk regions and countries, it is particularly important to protect investments from damage or loss, either by limiting hazard exposure or by reducing vulnerability. Risks of damage and loss should also be taken into account when estimating economic returns during project preparation. Owing to intersectoral interactions, large-scale covariate losses across multiple sectors can affect economic performance, even if those losses are concentrated in sectors outside a particular investment project.

The theory of risk used in this report to identify disaster risks at the global scale can be applied to more localized areas, as demonstrated by the case studies in the previous section. Similarly, the general methodology of estimating hazard exposure and vulnerabilities can be applied to identify various risks more precisely at national, subnational, and local scales. Such assessments can then be used to set standards and implement vulnerability reduction measures.

Sector Investment Operations. Investment project preparation, particularly in the high-risk areas identified in the global analysis, would benefit from including a risk assessment as a standard practice. This report's theory and methods can be translated easily into terms of reference for such assessments. Such assessments should identify probable hazards, as well as their spatial distribution and temporal characteristics (including return periods), and should evaluate vulnerabilities to the identified hazards that should be addressed in the project design.

Risk Reduction Operations. In high-risk countries and areas within countries, repeated, large-scale loss events can harm economic performance (Benson and Clay 2004). It may be impossible to achieve development goals such as poverty alleviation in these areas without concerted efforts to reduce recurrent losses. Increasingly, risk and loss reduction are being seen as investments in themselves, and disaster-prone countries are demonstrating a willingness to undertake projects in which disaster and loss reduction are the principal aims. Such projects can include both hard and soft components: measures to reduce the vulnerability and exposure of infrastructure, as well as emergency funds, institutional, policy, and capacity-building measures designed to increase the abilities of countries to manage disaster risks.

Countries with high disaster risks are candidates for these types of projects. Such countries may already experience frequent disasters and significant losses. They may require financial assistance such as periodic and perhaps frequent restructuring of their development portfolio to meet emergency needs, frequent emergency borrowing, or both. In such cases, disaster risk reduction projects offer a rational alternative to recurrent, unplanned emergency spending.

Contingency Financing. Emergency recovery and reconstruction needs after a major disaster may create a high demand for emergency financing. While such loans are usually appraised and approved relatively quickly, at times there can be delays in disbursing the funds, which increases the social and economic impacts of the disaster.

In urgent disaster situations, there is little time to plan the allocation of resources for cost-effective risk management over the longer term. Typically, a token amount of emergency funding is earmarked for "disaster preparedness," but risk reduction is not necessarily woven into the fabric of the reconstruction effort. At worst, hastily planned reconstruction can simply result in rebuilding the same risks that led to the disaster in the first place.

Advance planning for recovery and resource allocation would allow for better targeting of resources toward investments that would restore economic activity quickly and relieve human suffering. This report's global disaster risk analysis provides a basis for identifying situations in which future emergency recovery loans are likely to be needed. This creates an opportunity for "pre-appraising" emergency loans, that is, designing a risk management strategy to guide the allocation of emergency reconstruction resources should such resources become necessary, or to arrange for other types of contingency financing with development banks.

The exercise of identifying risks and risk management opportunities would have benefits even if emergency assistance is never needed, as it would create a road map for reducing disaster risks. If a disaster did occur, the availability of an "off-the-shelf" recovery package would avoid starting the emergency loan appraisal process from scratch and could identify previously planned risk reduction measures.

Information Development for Disaster Risk Management

The Hotspots project provides a common framework for improving risk identification and promoting risk management through a dialogue between organizations and individuals operating at various geographic scales. The methods and results provide useful tools for integrating disaster risk management into development efforts and should be developed further.

There is growing recognition of the need for better data and information on hazards and disasters at both national and international levels. Within the United States, several recent reports by the U.S. National Research Council (NRC) and the U.S. government have highlighted the importance of both historical and current data on hazard events and their associated impacts (NRC 1999a, 1999b; Subcommittee on Disaster Reduction 2003). At the international level, there is strong interest in improvement in disaster information systems and associated decision support tools (for example, ISDR 2003).

A welcome shift in emphasis appears to be under way from managing disasters by managing emergencies to managing disaster risks. This shift is evident in recent publications such as the *2002 World Disasters Report: Focus on Reducing Risk* (IFRC 2002), *Living with Risk* (ISDR 2004), *and Reducing Disaster Risk: A Challenge for Development* (UNDP 2004). Risk assessment, reduction, and transfer are the major elements of risk management (Kreimer and others 1999), offering a desirable alternative to managing disasters through emergency response. Risk reduction requires risk assessment in order to determine which areas are at highest risk of disaster and why, so that appropriate and cost-effective mitigation measures can be identified, adapted, and implemented.

We have designed the hotspots approach to be open-ended to allow additional studies to be incorporated on an ongoing basis. As a global analysis conducted with very limited local-level participation and based on incomplete data, the results presented here should not provide the sole basis for designing risk management activities. The analysis does, however, provide a scientific basis for understanding where risks are highest and why, as well as a methodological framework for regional- and local-scale analysis. The identified risks then can be evaluated further using more detailed data in the context of a region's or country's overall development strategy and priorities. The hotspots analysis can be improved upon as a tool and developed in several directions.

Improve Underlying Databases. The first direction is to pursue the many opportunities in both the short and long term to improve the underlying databases for assessing disaster risks and losses. A range of new global-scale data sets is currently under development, including a new global urban-extent database being developed by CIESIN in support of the Millennium Ecosystem Assessment. A joint project between the Earth Institute, the World Bank, and the Millennium Project will develop a much more detailed and complete database on subnational poverty and hunger. Much more comprehensive regional data sets will become available in specific areas of interest. On a regional scale, there are also much longer records of hazard events for specific hazards that could be harnessed to improve estimates of hazard frequency and intensity in high-risk areas (for example, O'Loughlin and Lander 2003). Significant improvements could be made in characterizing flood, drought, and landslide hazards in particular. Existing data on disaster-related losses are being compiled into a multitiered system through which regularly updated historical data from multiple sources can be accessed. Additional work to link and cross-check existing data is needed, however, as is improvement in the assessment and documentation of global economic losses.

Undertake Case Studies. A second direction is to explore more fully the applicability and utility of the hotspots approach to analysis and decision making at regional, national, and local scales. The initial case studies are promising, but they are certainly not on their own sufficient to demonstrate the value of the overall approach or the specific data and methods under different conditions. More direct involvement of potential stakeholders would be valuable in extending the approach to finer scales of analysis and decision making. To be effective, efforts to improve risk identification in hotspot areas should be part of a complete package of technical and financial support for the full range of measures needed to manage risks, including risk reduction and transfer.

Explore Long-term Trends. A third direction is to explore a key long-term issue: the potential effect of underlying changes in hazard frequency (for example, due to human-induced climatic change) coupled with long-term trends in human development and settlement patterns. To what degree could changes in tropical storm frequency, intensity, and tracks interact with continued coastal development (both urban and rural) to increase risks of death and destruction in these regions? Are agricultural areas, already under pressure from urbanization and other land use changes, likely to become more or less susceptible to drought, severe weather, or floods? Could other hazards such as wildfires potentially interact with changing patterns of drought, landslides, deforestation, and land use to create new types of hotspots? Although some aspects of these questions have been addressed in the general context of research on climate change impacts, the interactions between climate change, the full range of hazards, and evolving human hazard vulnerability have not been fully explored (for example, Brooks and Adger 2003; Chen 1994).

Pursuing work in these directions will necessarily involve a wide range of institutions—national, regional and international, public and private sector, academic, and operational. We hope that the Hotspots project has contributed a building block in the foundation of a global effort to reduce disaster-related losses by managing risks rather than by managing emergencies. We look forward to continuing collaboration with partners at all levels to put in place a global disaster risk management support system in order to mobilize the knowledge and resources necessary to achieve this goal.

Appendix A:
Technical Appendix for Global Analysis

A.1 Derivation of Tropical Cyclone, GDP Surfaces, and Agricultural Value

Tropical Cyclones

Data Sources:

UNEP: http://www.grid.unep.ch/data/grid/gnv200.php

Wind speed profile model: http://www.bbsr.edu/rpi/meetpart/land/holland2.html

Tracks of tropical cyclones are available from several different centers. UNEP assembled a data set of all the wind storms that occurred from 1981 through 2000. Wind speed profile models are used to delineate buffer zones around the track of a tropical cyclone. Hence the buffer zones represent the areas affected by the tropical cyclone. After evaluating different wind speed profile models, the model of Greg Holland was chosen (Holland 1997). This model was also used by UNEP to generate asymmetric wind speed profiles.

The different wind speed buffers are translated into six categories using the Saffir Simpson Hurricane scale. The globe was divided into small cells of one square kilometer. Overlaying the translated wind speed buffer zones of the storms that occurred in a given year with the one-kilometer resolution grid results in a surface that represents how often a grid cell is hit and the associated wind speed category. A combination of the yearly surfaces gives a global tropical cyclone frequency grid for the available data during 1981 through 2000.

Table A1.1. Available Tropical Cyclone Data by Region

Region	Data Availability
Atlantic Ocean	1981–2000
Australia	1984–2000
Indian Ocean, North	1992–1997, 1999–2000
Indian Ocean, South	1981–2000
Pacific Ocean, Northeast	1988–2000
Pacific Ocean, Northwest	1981–2000
Pacific Ocean, South	1981–2000

Global GDP Surface

Data Sources GDP:

CIESIN: http://sedac.ciesin.columbia.edu/plue/gpw/index.html?main.html&2

CIA Factbook: http://www.cia.gov/cia/publications/factbook/

World Development Indicators: http://www.worldbank.org/data/wdi2000/

All available subnational GDP data (preferably purchasing power parity [PPP] corrected, 2000) were collected for the world. Since these data come from different sources, the subnational data were used only to calculate the share of the national GDP of a subnational unit. The World Bank Indicators were used as a uniform data source for the national, PPP adjusted GDP in 2000.

The reallocation of the GDP to a subnational unit was based on the population distribution in that unit. The population in 2000 was projected based on CIESIN population database for 1995. These population numbers were adjusted at national level using the U.N. population numbers for the year 2000. The result is a global dollar value surface with a five-kilometer cell resolution based on the GDP.

Agricultural Value

Data Sources:

GLCCD: http://edcdaac.usgs.gov/glcc/glcc.asp

IFPRI: http://www.ifpri.org/pubs/books/page/agroeco_use.pdf

FAOSTATS: http://apps.fao.org/page/collections?subset=agriculture

The International Food Policy Research Institute (IFPRI) reinterpreted the Global Land Cover Characteristics Dataset of 1998 focusing on the agricultural area in every cell of the global one-kilometer resolution grid. A cell value represents the percentage of area in that cell used for agricultural purposes. The total agricultural area of a country was calculated.

Table A1.2. Subnational GDP Data

Argentina	Chile	United Kingdom	Korea, Rep. of	Romania
Australia	China	Greece	Lithuania	Russian Fed.
Austria	Colombia	Hungary	Latvia	Slovak Rep.
Belgium	Czech Rep.	Indonesia	Mexico	Slovenia
Bangladesh	Germany	India	Mozambique	Sweden
Bulgaria	Denmark	Ireland	Netherlands	Thailand
Bolivia	Spain	Iran, the Islamic Rep. of	Peru	Turkey
Brazil	Estonia	Italy	Philippines	United States
Canada	Finland	Japan	Poland	Vietnam
France	Kazakhstan	Portugal	South Africa	Switzerland

Production numbers for a specific crop in a country in 2000 come from the FAO Statistical Database (FAOSTATS). Multiplying these production numbers by IFPRI price per unit from 1989 through 1991 and summing them gives the total agricultural value of a country. This value was redistributed spatially over the agricultural area in a country to generate the agricultural value surface.

A.2 Reclassification of Hazardous Areas Weighted by Exposure

To characterize the effect of population density on the global distribution of hazard, we divide our grid cells into deciles based on population density and use the resulting index (1–10) to weight each hazard individually. A grid cell with a drought decile value of 8 might therefore have a drought-population index ranging from 8 to 80. Figures A2.1a–f illustrate the results for each hazard, using the same grouping of deciles for the population-weighted indexes as for the hazard-only indexes (red indicates the top three deciles, green the next three deciles, and blue the bottom four deciles).

For cyclones, there is a slight expansion of high-hazard areas in the Caribbean and the southeastern United States, in coastal areas of China, and in southern Africa. A few small areas in eastern India and Bangladesh also move into the highest three deciles under the influence of high population density. Flood areas also increase in most regions, at the expense of some relatively less densely populated areas along the U.S. Gulf Coast. Drought areas no longer considered as significant in terms of population density include parts of the western United States, interior South America, Kazakhstan, and southern Australia. Only minor changes are evident for volcanoes.

A more noticeable difference is evident for the earthquake data, which demonstrate a clear shift towards more densely populated areas of the northeast United States, Europe, the coast of West Africa, India, China, and the Koreas. Less populated areas, such as western South America, Indonesia, and New Zealand, rank lower on this scale.

Figure A2.1. Single-Hazard Exposure Index Based on Top Three Population-Weighted Deciles
a) Cyclones

Cyclone Hazard Exposure
Population Weighted Deciles

1st – 4th
5th – 7th
8th – 10th

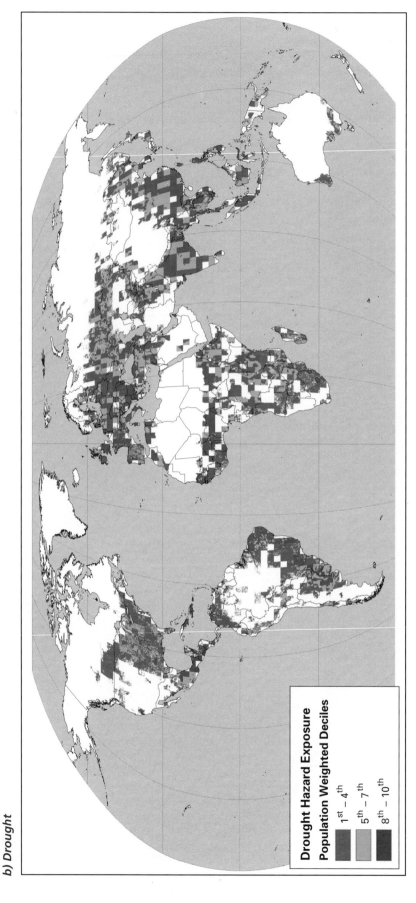

Figure A2.1. Single-Hazard Exposure Index Based on Top Three Population-Weighted Deciles
b) Drought

Figure A2.1. Single-Hazard Exposure Index Based on Top Three Population-Weighted Deciles.
c) Floods

Flood Hazard Exposure
Population Weighted Deciles

1st – 4th
5th – 7th
8th – 10th

Figure A2.1. Single-Hazard Exposure Index Based on Top Three Population-Weighted Deciles
d) Earthquakes (pga)

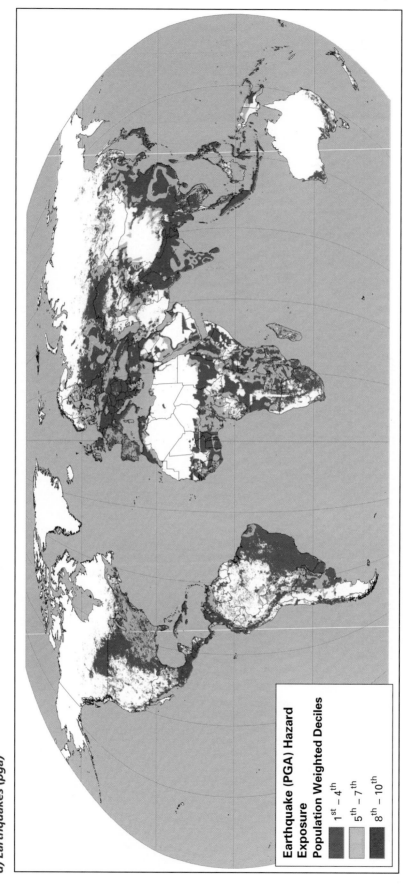

Earthquake (PGA) Hazard Exposure Population Weighted Deciles

1st – 4th

5th – 7th

8th – 10th

Figure A2.1. Single-Hazard Exposure Index Based on Top Three Population-Weighted Deciles

e) Volcanoes

Volcano Hazard Exposure
Population Weighted Deciles

1st – 4th
5th – 7th
8th – 10th

Figure A2.1. Single-Hazard Exposure Index Based on Top Three Population-Weighted Deciles
f) Landslides

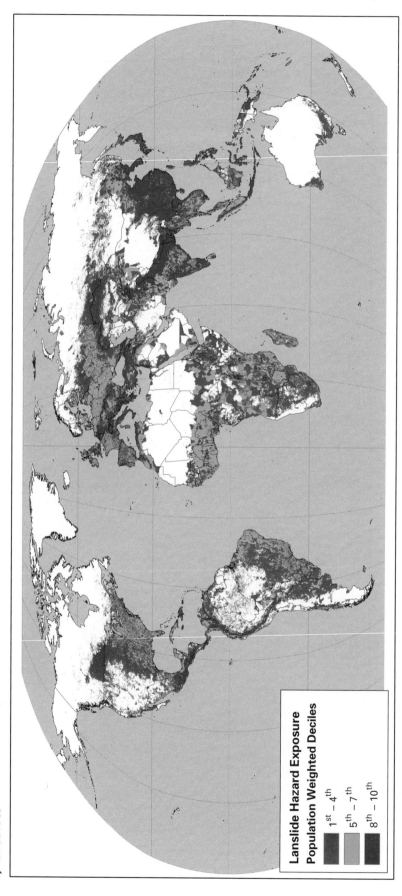

Lanslide Hazard Exposure
Population Weighted Deciles

1st – 4th
5th – 7th
8th – 10th

A.3 World Bank Country Income Classifications

Table A3.1. World Bank Country Income Classifications: High Income

European Monetary Union (12)		OECD (24)		Others, non-OECD (28)	
Country	2000 GDP (Millions of Current US$)	Country	2000 GDP (Millions of Current US$)	Country	2000 GDP (Millions of Current US$)
Austria	202,954	Australia	410,590	Andorra	..
Belgium	247,634	Austria	202,954	Aruba	..
Finland	130,797	Belgium	247,634	Bahamas, The	..
France	1,409,604	Canada	715,692	Bahrain	
Germany	1,976,240	Denmark	174,798	Bermuda	
Greece	132,834	Finland	130,797	Brunei	..
Ireland	119,916	France	1,409,604	Cayman Islands	..
Italy	1,180,921	Germany	1,976,240	Channel Islands	
Luxembourg	20,062	Greece	132,834	Cyprus	..
Netherlands	413,741	Iceland	8,608	Faeroe Islands	
Portugal	121,291	Ireland	119,916	French Polynesia	..
Spain	649,792	Italy	1,180,921	Greenland	..
		Japan	3,978,782	Guam	
		Korea, Rep. of	476,690	Hong Kong, China	161,532
		Luxembourg	20,062	Israel	..
		Netherlands	413,741	Kuwait	..
		New Zealand	58,178	Liechtenstein	
		Norway	189,436	Macao, China	
		Portugal	121,291	Monaco	..
		Spain	649,792	Netherlands Antilles	..
		Sweden	229,772	New Caledonia	..
		Switzerland	268,041	Northern Mariana Islands	
		United Kingdom	1,552,437	Qatar	..
		United States	10,416,820	San Marino	
				Singapore	86,969
				Slovenia	21,108
				United Arab Emirates	..
				Virgin Islands (U.S.)	..

Table A3.2. World Bank Country Income Classifications: Low and Middle Income

Low Income (65)		Lower Middle Income (52)		Upper Middle Income (38)	
Country	2000 GDP (Millions of Current US$)	Country	2000 GDP (Millions of Current US$)	Country	2000 GDP (Millions of Current US$)
Afghanistan	..	Albania	4,695	American Samoa	-
Angola	11,380	Algeria	55,666	Antigua and Barbuda	710
Armenia	2,367	Belarus	14,304	Argentina	102,191
Azerbaijan	6,090	Belize	843	Barbados	..
Bangladesh	47,328	Bolivia	7,678	Botswana	5,188
Benin	2,690	Bosnia and Herzegovina	5,249	Brazil	452,387
Bhutan	594	Bulgaria	15,608	Chile	64,154
Burkina Faso	2,839	Cape Verde	631	Costa Rica	16,887
Burundi	719	China	1,237,145	Croatia	22,421
Cambodia	3,677	Colombia	82,194	Czech Rep.	69,590
Cameroon	9,060	Cuba	..	Dominica	254
Central African Rep.	1,075	Djibouti	597	Estonia	6,413
Chad	1,935	Dominican Rep.	21,285	Gabon	4,971
Comoros	256	Ecuador	24,347	Grenada	414
Congo, Dem. Rep. of	5,704	Egypt, Arab Rep.	89,845	Hungary	65,843
Congo, Rep.	3,014	El Salvador	14,287	Isle of Man	-
Côte d'Ivoire	11,717	Fiji	1,878	Latvia	8,406
Equatorial Guinea	2,173	Guatemala	23,252	Lebanon	17,294
Eritrea	582	Guyana	710	Libya	..
Ethiopia	5,989	Honduras	6,594	Lithuania	13,796
Gambia, The	388	Iran, the Islamic Rep. of	107,522	Malaysia	95,157
Georgia	3,324	Iraq	..	Malta	..
Ghana	6,021	Jamaica	8,001	Mauritius	4,532
Guinea	3,174	Jordan	9,296	Mayote	-
Guinea-Bissau	216	Kazakhstan	24,205	Mexico	637,205
Haiti	3,590	Kiribati	44	Oman	20,073
India	515,012	Macedonia, FYR	3,712	Palau	130
Indonesia	172,911	Maldives	618	Panama	12,296
Kenya	12,140	Marshall Islands	108	Poland	187,680
Korea, Dem. People's Rep. of	..	Micronesia, Fed. Sts.	232	Puerto Rico	..
Kyrgyz Rep.	1,632	Morocco	37,263	Saudi Arabia	..
Lao People's Dem. Rep. of	1,680	Namibia	2,793	Seychelles	630
Lesotho	730	Paraguay	5,389	Slovak Rep.	23,700
Liberia	564	Peru	56,901	St. Kitts and Nevis	340
Madagascar	4,514	Philippines	77,076	St. Lucia	660
Malawi	1,880	Romania	44,428	Trinidad and Tobago	9,372
Mali	3,163	Russian Federation	346,520	Uruguay	12,325
Mauritania	983	Samoa	261	Venezuela	94,340
Moldova	1,621	South Africa	104,235		
Mongolia	1,262	Sri Lanka	16,373		
Mozambique	3,920	St. Vincent and Grenadines	361		
Nepal	5,493	Suriname	895		
Nicaragua	..	Swaziland	1,177		
Niger	2,170	Syrian Arab Rep.	21,872		
Nigeria	43,540	Thailand	126,407		
Pakistan	60,521	Tonga	136		
Papua New Guinea	2,793	Tunisia	21,169		
Rwanda	1,736	Turkey	182,848		
São Tomé and Principe	50	Turkmenistan	7,672		
Senegal	4,940	Vanuatu	234		
Sierra Leone	789	West Bank and Gaza	3,015		
Solomon Islands	240	Yugoslavia, Fed. Rep. (Serbia/Montenegro)	15,555		
Somalia	..				

continued

Table A3.2. continued

Low Income (65)		Lower Middle Income (52)		Upper Middle Income (38)	
Country	*2000 GDP (Millions of Current US$)*	*Country*	*2000 GDP (Millions of Current US$)*	*Country*	*2000 GDP (Millions of Current US$)*
Sudan	13,490				
Tajikistan	1,208				
Tanzania	9,383				
Timor-Leste	388				
Togo	1,384				
Uganda	5,866				
Ukraine	41,380				
Uzbekistan	9,713				
Vietnam	35,110				
Yemen, Rep. of	10,395				
Zambia	3,683				
Zimbabwe	8,304				

References

Advanced National Seismic System. 1997. Composite Earthquake Catalog. Available at http://quake.geo.berkeley.edu/anss/ (accessed December 2003).

Benson, C., and E. J. Clay. 2004. *Understanding the Economic and Financial Impacts of Natural Disasters*. Disaster Risk Management Series No. 4. Washington, DC: The World Bank. 134 pp. Available at http://www.wds.worldbank.org/servlet/WDS_IBank_Servlet?pcont=details&eid=000012009_20040420135752.

Brooks, N., and W. N. Adger. 2003. Country level risk measures of climate-related natural disasters and implications for adaptation to climate change. Working Paper 26, Tyndall Center for Climate Change Research. Norwich, UK: University of East Anglia. 25 pp.

Burton, I., R. W. Kates, and G. F. White. 1993. *The Environment as Hazard.* 2d Ed. New York: Guilford Press.

Center for International Earth Science Information Network (CIESIN), Columbia University; International Food Policy Research Institute (IFPRI); and World Resources Institute (WRI). 2000. *Gridded Population of the World (GPW), Version 2.* Palisades, NY: CIESIN, Columbia University. Available at http://sedac.ciesin.columbia.edu/plue/gpw.

Center for International Earth Science Information Network (CIESIN), Columbia University; International Center for Research on Tropical Agriculture (CIAT). 2004. Gridded Population of the World (GPW), Version 3 (beta). Palisades, NY: CIESIN, Columbia University. Available at http://beta.sedac.ciesin.columbia.edu/gpw.

Chen, R. S. 1994. The human dimension of vulnerability. In *Industrial Ecology and Global Change,* R. Socolow, C. Andrews, F. Berkhout, and V. Thomas, eds. Cambridge, UK: Cambridge University Press. pp. 85–105.

Center for International Earth Science Information Network: http://sedac.ciesin.columbia.edu/plue/gpw/index.html?main.html&2

Central Intelligence Agency Factbook. 2004. Washington, D.C. Available at http://www.cia.gov/cia/publications/factbook

Coburn, A. W., R. J. S. Spence, and A. Pomonis. 1994. *Vulnerability and Risk Assessment.* 2d Ed. Disaster Management Training Programme. New York: United Nations Development Programme. 69 pp.

Economic Commission for Latin America and the Caribbean (ECLAC) and the World Bank. 2003. *Handbook for Estimating the Socio-Economic and Environmental Effects of Disasters.* Mexico City and Washington, DC: ECLAC and the World Bank.

Gaffin, S. R., C. Rosenzweig, X. Xing, and G. Yetman. 2004. Downscaling and geo-spatial gridding of socioeconomic projections from the IPCC Special Report on Emissions Scenarios (SRES). *Global Environmental Change* 14(2): 105–123.

Holland, G. 1997. Horizontal wind structure. Paper presented at the Workshop on Windfield Dynamics of Landfalling Tropical Cyclones, 28–30 May 1997. Available at http://www.bbsr.edu/rpi/meetpart/land/holland2.html (accessed 30 August 2004).

Hubert-Ferrari, A., A. Barka, E. Jacques, S. S. Nalbant, B. Meyer, R. Armijo, P. Tapponnier, and J. P. King. 2000. Seismic hazard in the Marmara Sea region following the 17 August 1999 Izmit earthquake. *Nature* 404: 269.